$ 95

STRAIGHT FROM THE HEART

JOHN E. COCKAYNE, JR.

Straight from the Heart

John Bertolucci
with
John Blattner

SERVANT BOOKS
Ann Arbor, Michigan

Cover photo and design by Michael Andaloro

Published by Servant Books
P.O. Box 8617
Ann Arbor, Michigan 48107

Printed in the United States of America
ISBN 0-89283-290-8

86 87 88 89 90 91   10 9 8 7 6 5 4 3 2 1

Dedication

THIS BOOK IS DEDICATED TO DANIEL FERGUSON who fell asleep in the Lord on December 26, 1984, in his eighteenth year of life. He witnessed to me in a powerful way that "While we live we are responsible to the Lord, and when we die we die as His servants. Both in life and in death we are the Lord's" (Rom 14:8).

I also dedicate this work to the countless young people who have inspired and challenged me to become a better man of God. I honor the youth I have encountered during my ministry within the Diocese of Albany, New York, and those I presently serve through the ministries of The Franciscan University of Steubenville, the St. Francis Association for Catholic Evangelism, and the evangelistic outreach of FIRE.

Let no one look down on you because of your youth, but be a continuing example of love, faith, and purity to believers.
(1 Tm 4:12)

For your salvation I offer my life to Him who is Forever Young.

John P. Bertolucci
Priest

Contents

Introduction

I MET FR. JOHN BERTOLUCCI FOURTEEN YEARS AGO when we ministered together at a workshop on Inner Healing at a Notre Dame Conference. We have continued to work closely together in conferences and rallies as well as in our shared life and mission together at the campus of The Franciscan University of Steubenville.

Fr. John has consistently exhibited great interest in and love for young people. They flock around him on campus. They are drawn to him from brief encounters in the course of our travels. He listens. He loves. He speaks truth to them. Then he recounts the stories of his great experiences with them. I hear them at the dinner table, on airplanes, in Fr. John's homilies, and at the rallies we do together.

Now you can read the stories and meet Douglas, Patrick, Mark, Sandy, Joe, Carol and the rest. You can experience their lives and learn to love them as Fr. John does. You can get inside Fr. John's heart and mind as he cares for them, and you can receive the teachings that he developed to deal with their lives and the lives of young people throughout the world.

Read this book and discover for the first time or the hundredth time that Jesus is the answer to the struggles of our lives. Find the depth of your personal relationship with Jesus, Savior and Lord. Maybe you will express it as Patrick did, "Jesus, my friend."

Michael Scanlan, T.O.R.
President, Franciscan University
of Steubenville

ONE

"Please Bury Me"

ANNE, MY SECRETARY, sounded worried.

"Excuse me, Father, but Douglas is on the phone. He doesn't sound good."

"Thanks. I'll take it."

I paused for a moment before picking up the receiver, mentally "shifting gears" from sermon preparation to psychological counseling. Douglas was a young man I had been working with, on and off, for a couple of years. Doug had a lot going for him. He was eighteen, intelligent, good-looking, artistic. But he had managed to encounter quite an array of problems in his short life. Many young people struggle with drugs, alcohol, and personal relationships, not to mention the stress of finding their identity in a very confused society.

He had been in to see me just the day before, our first visit in almost a year. I had been weary and distracted—he had caught me on "one of those days"—and our conversation was not very productive. I had told him to call me so we could set up another time to get together later in the week.

I punched the blinking button on my phone.

"Hello? Father John?"

The voice sounded small, weak, and far away—almost *faded*, as if it were coming from beneath a great mountain of weariness. I had heard that voice before.

"Yes, Doug. This is me."

"Father John . . . please bury me."

The line went dead.

"Doug? Where are you? Doug!" I clicked the receiver frantically, but it was no use. He had hung up.

Please bury me. I felt as though the bottom had fallen out of my stomach. I had studied enough psychological counseling as part of my training for the priesthood to recognize a suicide call when I heard one.

"Call Doug's parents," I shouted to Anne as I rushed out the door. "Their work numbers are in the file somewhere. And call the police, too. Tell them to get to Doug's house right away. I'm afraid he's going to hurt himself."

Please bury me. My mind was reeling as I sped down the highway with my emergency lights flashing. Scenes from conversations and confrontations I'd had with Douglas flashed through my mind. "Don't do it, Doug. Please don't do it," I whispered as I drove. Then, "Jesus, please don't let him do it. Please, Lord. Let me get there in time."

Some time ago, Douglas had been referred to me for counseling. He was seventeen then, just out of high school. Like most people who begin seeing a counselor, he couldn't put his finger on what was bothering him. Although he was very bright and had always done fairly well in school, his grades were slipping. He was handsome, a good athlete, well-liked at school, and he had a girlfriend of whom he was very fond. Yet he had lost interest in living. He was depressed, lonely, and confused, and he didn't know what to do about it.

One part of his problem became obvious almost immediately. Doug was a regular user of marijuana.

It had started out innocently enough: trying "pot" just to see what it was like. But over time, as he found it more and more difficult to cope with the hassles that came with being a teenager, his use of marijuana increased.

I tried to tell Doug that using such a drug would alter his personality and undermine his ability to cope with life. But he claimed to know what he was doing. He said he had everything under control. Scientific studies, he said, "proved" that marijuana had no harmful effects. So what was so wrong about "smoking a little grass"?

Yet I could see clearly how Doug's drug use was compounding all his other problems. Patiently, repeatedly, I tried to get him to see what he was doing to himself, but he wouldn't listen.

He also ignored anything I told him about Jesus Christ. Even more than his use of drugs, I knew that his deep spiritual void held him back. More than anything else, he needed to let God come into his life.

At first he humored me. He would sit there and smile at me, listening politely to what I had to say, and then shrug it all off. I could almost read his thoughts. *You're a priest. You're supposed to say all that stuff. What do you know about young people and our problems?*

As time went on, he more and more resisted my efforts to share the Lord with him. He had swallowed the propaganda of our modern culture. He believed that men and women don't need God, that they can make it on their own, that religion is just a crutch. It got to the point where I would simply mention the name "Jesus," and he would snap, "Don't start in on that church stuff again." Then all I could do was retreat into a proper, professional, therapist-to-client style of relating. After he would leave, I would plead with God to somehow break through into Douglas's mixed-up life.

This went on for about a year. Doug actually showed some signs of improvement. The depression that had plagued him seemed to have lifted a little. He was doing better in school. He was handling his relationships with other people better. He had even cut back his use of marijuana somewhat. When the time came for me to be transferred to another assignment, it seemed alright to me, and to the people who were supervising my handling of Doug's case, to terminate our formal counseling relationship.

At least, it seemed alright from a *professional* point of view. Spiritually, a lot more needed to happen in Doug's life. Despite his progress, he had never definitely committed his life to Jesus Christ. Without that, I knew, he could never be completely healed and restored. I continued to pray for him.

Then, almost a year after our last meeting, he had appeared unannounced at my office. I winced now as I recalled our meeting, and the traumatic circumstances that had preceded it.

It was Sunday. I finished my masses in the morning and then took my parents out to dinner to celebrate their anniversary. We went to our favorite place, an Italian restaurant on one of the city's main thoroughfares.

During dinner, I happened to glance out the window onto the busy street. As I did, I noticed an elderly woman coming out of the laundromat next door. She had a bag of laundry under one arm and a sack of groceries under the other. Perhaps because she had so much to carry, she didn't go to the crosswalk at the corner but simply cut between two parked cars and started across the street. She hadn't seen the car speeding through the yellow light at the intersection. As I watched in horror, the car struck her head on and threw her to the pavement.

I was out of my chair in a flash. "Call an ambulance," I shouted at the restaurant cashier. "There's been an accident."

I rushed outside, with my father right behind me. He held up traffic while I knelt there in the middle of the street and tried to help the woman. She was obviously badly injured. Medically, there was nothing I could do for her. But I told her I was a priest, and as we waited for the ambulance to arrive I helped her make her peace with God. Then she lost consciousness.

After I drove my parents home, I went to the hospital and paced outside the emergency room as the doctors tried to save the elderly woman's life. But her injuries were too serious. She died without regaining consciousness.

I was emotionally drained. I went back home, needing some time to myself, time to pray and to rest. I was sitting in my study, still shaken from the experience, when Douglas walked in.

He was in bad shape.

It had to do with his girlfriend—or, rather, with his fiancée; they had gotten engaged a few months earlier. Their relationship had always been rocky. In fact, it had been one of our more frequent topics of conversation when we were meeting together regularly.

The main problem was Doug's possessiveness. Even more than drugs, he looked upon his relationship with his girlfriend as his main source of security, his source of ultimate meaning in life. The more he pinned his security on her, the more dependent he became and the more he began to act as if he owned her.

For a while, sensing his need and sincerely wanting to help him, she was able to bear with him. But before long she realized that Doug's difficulties were more serious than she had thought and they were growing worse. Every time it looked as though he was finally getting on top of his problems, there would be a relapse. He would get depressed and moody. The clinging dependence and suffocating possessiveness would start all over again.

Eventually, it was just too much for her. The morning of the day Doug came to see me she had called him to say she couldn't go through with the wedding. The engagement was off, and their relationship was on hold until he could get his act together.

I had no question that this was the right thing for her to do. Doug could never make a marriage work in his emotional and psychological condition. Perhaps, I thought to myself, breaking the engagement was the most loving thing to do in the long run, even though it was certainly painful in the short run. It might force Doug to face up to his problems instead of using the relationship to compensate for them.

All that would take time, I realized. For now, the main thing was to help Doug through his immediate crisis.

Unfortunately, I wasn't doing very well at that. I was still shaken up from what had happened earlier that afternoon. All I could think was, "Oh, Lord. Twelve months of counseling, and now it's just blowing up in my face. Why? Why *today*, of all days?" I did my best to listen to what Doug was saying and to respond as helpfully as I could; but we weren't getting anywhere.

After an hour or so he had calmed down somewhat. As he got up to leave, I apologized for my distraction and urged him to call me the next day so we could set up a time to get together and talk some more. I thought that was why he was calling when my secretary interrupted my sermon preparation to tell me he was on the line.

Please bury me. Those three words echoed in my ears as I finally neared Doug's house. His family lived just outside of town.

As I swerved around the last bend in the road, I could see the policemen jumping out of their patrol car. His parents were just arriving, too, pulling into the driveway right behind me.

Please, Lord, I prayed for the thousandth time as I got out of my car and ran up the front walk. *Please don't let him do anything. Please let us get to him first.*

I was there when they found him.

He was sprawled in the grass behind the house. He had shot himself once in the head.

Amazingly, he was still alive. I knelt down beside him and prayed as family and paramedics tried to help him. I felt like screaming at him. *Doug! Why? How could you do something like this?* But as he looked up at me through frightened eyes, I knew it was no time for anger. For the second time in two days, I was being called upon to help a wounded, frightened human being make peace with God and prepare to meet him face to face. I led Douglas through the same prayer I had led the elderly woman through the day before, the prayer I had longed to lead him through so many times before.

Lord Jesus Christ, I love you. I am sorry for my sins. I accept you as my Savior and my Lord, and I surrender my life to you.

Tears began to stream down the side of Doug's cheeks as his eyes gazed into mine. *Why didn't I listen to you before?* they seemed to say. *Why did it come to this?*

As Douglas lay there in my arms, and as he internally prayed that prayer of repentance and commitment to the Lord Jesus Christ, I believe that Jesus came and knelt there beside him and, looking upon his heart, heard his prayer and forgave him.

I gave Douglas the last rites of the Roman Catholic Church. *I absolve you from your sins in the name of the Father, and of the Son, and of the Holy Spirit.* I placed the blessed oil on his forehead and commended his spirit to God. *Through this holy anointing may the Lord in His love and mercy help you with the grace of the Holy Spirit. May the Lord who frees you from sin save you and raise you up.* As the moment of death drew near I prayed the apostolic pardon, the final blessing of the Church. *Through the holy mysteries of our redemption, may Almighty God release you from all punishments in this life and in the life to come. May he open to you the gates of paradise and welcome you to everlasting joy.*

Two days later, I did what Douglas had asked me to do. I buried him. I presided at his funeral, and preached his eulogy, and led the graveside service at the cemetery.

It was a painful victory. A victory, because I knew Douglas was with the Lord. But a painful victory. Painful for his parents, whom I tried to console but who could not begin to understand the awful torment that had led their son to take his life. Painful for his girlfriend, who was overcome with guilt despite my reassurances that Doug's death was not her fault.

And painful for me, too, because I had loved Douglas, had prayed for him, fasted for him, wept for him. I waited until all the others had left the grave site, and watched until the last spadeful of earth had been thrown over his grave. Then I dropped to my knees and sobbed, crying out to God in my anguish over such a tragic, senseless loss.

Many of Doug's friends were at his funeral, and I addressed them directly in my sermon. I pleaded with them not to make the mistakes Doug had made. I pleaded with them, no matter how big or impossible their problems seemed to them, not to take the way out that Doug had chosen. Most of all, I pleaded with them not to miss out on the overwhelming love and acceptance and strength that was available to them in Jesus Christ.

As I knelt beside Douglas' grave, I promised myself and I promised the Lord that I would never pass up an opportunity to speak with young people about Jesus Christ. About the forgiveness he won for us on the cross. About the wisdom he offers us for every aspect of our lives. About the peace and joy he pours into our hearts through his Holy Spirit. About the great love he has for young people. And about the tremendous challenge he sets before them to serve him and hasten the coming of his kingdom.

TWO

"Jesus My Friend"

A S LONELY AS I FELT, weeping there beside Douglas' grave, I knew I was not alone. I knew there was another who knelt there beside me, who knew the same heartache I knew, who felt the same grief I felt, who shed the same tears I shed. As much as I loved Douglas, there was another who loved him even more. And as deeply as I now long to see other young men and women delivered from the tragic fate that came to Douglas, there is another who longs for it more deeply still.

Jesus Loves You

Please listen when I say to you: the Lord Jesus Christ loves you. He understands what you're going through. He knows the challenges you face, the problems you have, the feelings you struggle with.

He knows how many of you feel alone and afraid. He knows how many of you cry yourselves to sleep at night because of the fear and loneliness you experience. He knows how many of you struggle in your relationships with your parents, your teachers, your friends at school. He knows how many of you have been wounded by boyfriends and girlfriends, or perhaps by adults who have failed you in some way.

He knows how many of you have sought meaning and happiness in money, or clothes, or achievement. He knows

19

how many of you have been caught up in drinking, or drugs, or sex. He knows how many of you have felt trapped, thinking there is no way out. He knows how many of you have been tempted to end it all by taking your own life.

And he knows *you*. He doesn't just know the *kinds* of problems that young people like you face, but he knows the exact difficulties that you yourself are facing this very moment. He understands them. He has the solution for them. In fact, he *is* the solution for them. He came so that *you* might have life and have it in abundance. He gave us his word so that you could walk in his wisdom. He died so that your sins might be forgiven. He rose again so that you might find new life in him. He sent his Holy Spirit so that you could have peace and joy every day of your life.

Patrick's Story

Let me tell you the story of another young man whom the Lord brought into my life. I met him while I was ministering in a foreign country where I had been invited to speak at a Catholic high school.

The president of the senior class at this high school was a young man named Patrick. He didn't believe in God at all and was flirting with the idea of becoming a Marxist.

Patrick was a born leader. I guess he had to be, to be an atheist and still get elected president of the senior class in a Catholic high school. The moment I met him, I sensed the Lord saying to me, *I want this young man.*

I was going to say mass later that day, and I invited Patrick to come. He wasn't very interested. "I don't believe in any of that religious garbage," he told me through an interpreter. "I'll come, but only because the senior class is going and I'm the class president. I'll just stand off to the side until it's over."

That's just what he did, too. He stood off to one side of the church and stared up at the ceiling, looking bored.

Throughout the mass, Patrick kept coming to mind. I kept

remembering how the Lord had told me he wanted to bring Patrick to himself, so in between the formal prayers, I mentally prayed, "Come on, Lord! Get him!"

I wasn't the only one, either. I had asked a few of the other class members to pray for him as well. All over the room I could see them: young men and women, their lips murmuring silent prayers, glancing furtively at Patrick to see if anything was happening. Nothing was.

It was a tremendous liturgy: lively music, great singing, a strong sense of the presence of God. We moved through the readings, the sermon, the presentation of the bread and wine. Still nothing from Patrick. "Come on, Jesus!" I prayed. "Go get him!"

We reached the part of the mass where we pray the Lord's Prayer together. I looked over to where Patrick stood. A small group of young men had inconspicuously gathered around him. A couple, who were standing behind him where he couldn't see them, extended their hands over him as they prayed. *Thy kingdom come, thy will be done on earth as it is in heaven. . . .* "Lightning, Lord!" I prayed. "Let your lightning strike!"

I looked over at Patrick. He had dropped to his knees, sobbing. This big, tough, hard-boiled, thick-skinned, soccer-star class president was kneeling in the middle of all his friends and crying like a baby.

Why? Because Jesus Christ had embraced him. Jesus Christ had said to him, "Patrick, I love you. I love you so much I gave my life for you. No matter what you've done, I love you and I can cleanse you of every one of your sins."

One of the other priests went over and knelt down beside Patrick to hear his confession (which took quite a while). Then Patrick rose and went to receive communion for the first time in many years.

I was going the next day to visit an Indian mission station in the Andes mountains, and Patrick volunteered to drive me there in his jeep. It was quite a ride. The roads were very narrow and the mountains were very steep and there were no guardrails. And Patrick was still weeping, even as he drove the jeep at what I thought was an incredible rate of speed.

We had a hard time communicating. He could barely speak any English, and I could barely speak his language. At one point he turned toward me, tears streaming down his cheeks and his eyes so aglow they seemed to be on fire. I looked at him inquiringly, *Patrick, how are you doing? What's going on inside you? What is God doing in you?*

He understood what I wanted to ask. He choked out three words of broken English that told me everything I needed to know. "Father John," he said, "Jesus my friend."

Friendship with Jesus

Douglas' last words to me, "Please bury me," summed up the misery and despair of life apart from Jesus Christ. In the same way, "Jesus my friend," the three words of Patrick's sum up the kind of relationship the Lord wants to have with each one of us. He wants to be our friend. His friendship is not the weak, superficial kind of friendship we so often experience with other people, but one that is deep, strong, secure.

I've talked with numerous young people over the course of many years, and I know how many struggle with loneliness and rejection. But it doesn't matter how lonely you feel. It doesn't matter if you've never had a girlfriend or a boyfriend. It doesn't matter who has rejected you: your friends, your classmates, even your parents. Jesus loves you more than all of them put together ever could. He thinks you are special, and he loves you with a love that has no end. He wants to be your friend.

The Faithful Friend

We all want to be accepted by those around us, to feel that we are needed, that we belong. This is a very natural human desire. But sometimes it seems so strong that we let it become the driving force in our lives, pushing everything else into second place. Before long, we are living for the approval of others, pinning all our security and happiness on how others relate to us. When we do this, we are only setting ourselves up for disappointment.

How many of us have already found this out? We found someone who we thought would be our one true friend forever. We thought, "Great! Now I've got everything I've been looking for." Then, a little while later, something went wrong. The other person wasn't everything we thought they would be. The one we depended on let us down, and since our whole world was built around that one relationship, it seemed as though everything collapsed.

The simple fact is that no human relationship can provide for us what friendship with Jesus Christ is intended to provide. He is the faithful friend, the one who never lets us down. When we put our friendship with him first in our lives, all our other friendships can fall into proper perspective.

All of us know what it means to be lonely, to feel empty inside. And all of us try to hide it. Young people work especially hard to keep their inner emptiness from showing on the outside. They act cool. They pretend they have it all together. But even the coolest ones of all—if they don't know Jesus Christ—still go home and struggle with the emptiness inside.

And all the time Jesus stands before us, saying, "Won't you let me into your heart? I love you. I'm what you're searching for. I can take away the loneliness. I can fill the emptiness inside you. Let me be your friend."

Be Real with Jesus

I know what some of you are thinking: "Jesus doesn't want to be *my* friend. He couldn't love someone like me. He couldn't love someone who's done the things I've done. He couldn't love somebody as messed up as I am."

If you are thinking those kinds of thoughts, I've got good news for you. You can come to Jesus just as you are, with all your confusion, with all your emotional ups and downs, with all your struggles. You don't have to cover anything up. You don't have to play games. You don't have to pretend to be something you're not. You can be real with Jesus.

You can tell Jesus about your fears, your worries, your problems. You can tell him about your difficulties at home or at school. You can tell him about relationships that aren't working right. Even when something is bothering you and you can't put your finger on what it is, you can lay that before Jesus, too.

You can even be real with Jesus about your sins—even about the one you're most ashamed of, the one you've never told to your parents, or to your priest, or to your best friend. Tell it to Jesus. Open up your heart to him. Get all your skeletons out of the closet.

The fact is, he already knows what skeletons are in the closet. He knows all about your sins, and he knows that none of them are beyond the reach of his forgiveness. He is waiting for you to confess your sins to him so that he can cover them with his blood and help you know the joy and peace of his forgiveness. He will also give you the courage to confess those sins to his ordained representative.

The Only Way to Happiness

Almost two thousand years ago, Jesus hung on the cross. He bled, and suffered, and died, so that all our sins could be washed away, so that we could know the peace and joy that comes from being in fellowship with God.

He had done nothing wrong. He had harmed no one. He had come to preach a message of love and reconciliation. But, as John writes in his Gospel, "to his own he came, yet his own did not accept him" (Jn 1:11). He was crucified, and he died, and his body was laid in a tomb.

But three days later he rose from the dead, and he walked out of that tomb alive. By shedding his blood he paid the penalty for all the sins of all men and women for all time, including every sin that you and I have ever committed. By his dying, he conquered death and the power of evil, so that we "might be slaves to sin no longer" (Rom 6:6). By his rising again, he opened the way for you and me to enter into newness of life, and he showed, once and for all, that he is just what he said he is: the way, the truth, and the life.

No one else has ever said what Jesus said. No one else in the history of mankind has ever claimed to be the way, the truth, and the life. There are some who say, "Here is *a* way." And there are some who say, "Here is *some* truth." And there are some who say, "Vote for me, or buy my books, or follow my teachings, and I will help you improve your life." But Jesus said, "I am *the* way, *the* truth, and *the* life."

What does that mean? It means there is only one way to happiness. There is only one way to fulfillment. There is only one way to peace and joy. And that way is by giving our lives totally and completely to Jesus Christ.

"Enter through the narrow gate," Jesus said, speaking of himself. "The gate that leads to damnation is wide, the road is clear, and many choose to travel it. But how narrow is the gate that leads to life, how rough the road, and how few there are who actually find it" (Mt 7:13).

High on Jesus

Do you know what it's like to get high on Jesus? To wake up in the morning and to know that life is worth living because the Lord of all the universe loves you? To go through the day with a sense of dignity and purpose because God has called you to serve him and has sent his Spirit to live inside you? It's the greatest feeling in the world.

If you don't know that feeling, you can. Give your life to Jesus Christ. I'm not talking about becoming a priest or a minister or a nun or a missionary—though all those are excellent things to be. I'm talking about becoming a *disciple*. A disciple is one who follows, one who gives his life for the service of another. No matter whether you're old or young, single or married, in a job or still in school, you can be a disciple of Jesus Christ.

> "Hear O Israel! The Lord our God is Lord alone! Therefore you shall love the Lord your God with all your heart, with all your soul, with all your mind, and with all your strength."
> (Mk 12:29-30)

This passage—quoted by Jesus from the ancient Jewish Scriptures—represents the very heart of our Christian call. It is the "job description" of a disciple: to love the Lord with everything in us.

"I beg you through the mercy of God to offer your bodies as a living sacrifice holy and acceptable to God, your spiritual worship. Do not conform yourselves to this age but be transformed by the renewal of your mind, so that you may judge what is God's will, what is good, pleasing, and perfect" (Rom 12:1-2).

These words were originally addressed to the Christians at Rome by the apostle Paul, but they are equally addressed to all men and women by the Holy Spirit. More specifically, I address them to each one of you reading this book.

I beg you, and I challenge you, to offer the entirety of your being—body, mind, soul, and spirit—to Jesus Christ. Don't hold anything back. Give him everything you've got, everything you are, everything you ever hope to be.

Jesus Christ wants to be your friend. Even now he stands before you, waiting for you to invite him into your heart. Even now he walks up, puts his arms around you, and says, "I love you as though you were the only person on earth. I know what you're going through. I know all about your sin, your weakness, your pain, your loneliness. Give me the burdens you're carrying. Give me the problems you're struggling with. Tell me the sins that weigh you down with guilt, and I'll lift the weight of guilt from your shoulders. I'm here. I'm here and I love you. I'm here and I want to be your friend."

A Prayer of Repentance

Lord Jesus Christ, I acknowledge that I am a sinner. I grieve and weep to know that I have shared in causing your sufferings by my sin and rebellion.

But Lord, I confess my sins. I am truly sorry for my sins. I turn away from them and reach out to you, accepting you as my Lord and my God. I receive you into my life as my personal Savior.

I thank you, Lord, that your blood shed on the cross cleanses me of my sins and washes away my guilt. I thank you that you have given me the sacrament of reconciliation, so that I can confess my sins to an elder of the Church and hear the words of forgiveness. I thank you that I can come to your altar to renew my covenant with you through your very Body and Blood.

Christ Jesus, live within my heart. Help me know your mercy and forgiveness. Fill me with your Holy Spirit. Heal and strengthen me in every area of my life. Give me the grace to change for the better day by day by day, until that great day when I am united completely with you and your Father and the Holy Spirit in the world that will be without end.

Amen.

THREE

The Inside Story

I T'S ONE THING TO HEAR about the difficulties of being a young person in the modern world from someone like me, and another thing to hear about it from other young people. Of course, I was young once myself (it wasn't *all* that long ago), and I've talked with and counseled hundreds of high school and college students over the years. So I believe my impressions and observations are fairly reliable. But even so, you just can't beat a first hand report from someone who's right in the middle of the situation.

So, in this chapter, we're going to hear the inside story: what young people themselves have to say about their struggles and their relationship with Jesus. Not long ago I had the opportunity to spend some time with a group of high school and college-age people from the Christian Community of God's Delight, in Dallas, Texas. I asked them about the challenges they face in their daily lives, and about how their faith in Jesus Christ helps them deal with those challenges.

Fr. John: What are some of the difficulties that young people face today? Among the people you relate with at school, in your dormitories—what are some of the main struggles your friends are dealing with?

Joe: For the last couple of years, Mark and I have manned the religion table during pre-registration at our college. Lots of kids come through, and we're supposed to ask them what their religious preference is. Then we write that down on their registration card, so that churches or Christian groups can contact them and invite them to church or to a meeting. It's been really surprising to see how many students don't have any religious background.

Mark: Or, at least, none that matters to them. A lot of them just say, "Oh, Catholic, I guess." They might have some kind of church background, but it doesn't make any difference to them. And others are wandering around trying to find a set of beliefs, a value system that they feel comfortable with.

So a lot of them haven't yet "come in for a landing"? Do they seem to be interested or actively searching? Or are they just unconcerned about it?

Mark: Most just seem totally unconcerned. Others, you can tell, are searching for something, but they're not sure what.

I occasionally travel in Europe, and I always find it interesting to talk to young people over there. Their image of American youth isn't very good. They view young people in the United States as having a lot of problems. Would you agree with that? Would you say that American youth are facing major problems? Or is that an exaggerated view?

Carol: I think it's accurate. The biggest problem I see is that it's hard to find a friend that you can really count on. Somebody who thinks the same way you do, and who wants the same things in life that you want.

Mark: It's especially hard in college. People come from such diverse backgrounds. When you're in high school, everyone has pretty much the same socio-economic status, the same background. But in college, people are coming from all over the place. Some of what they bring with them is good and some of it is garbage. It's harder to find people who believe the same things you do.

You're faced, then, with the challenge of relating to people who are at different places in their lives. What struggles are they having?

Sandy: A lot of the students at my university are experiencing an identity crisis. They don't know what their values are, but now they're away from home, they have to decide for themselves what they're going to do or not do. Many of them have never had to do that before. Now they have to do it every day. They don't know what to base their decisions on, so they let their choices be formed by their environment, by the friends they happen to pick up, by the places they happen to be.

So peer influence is very important. If you hang around with people who are doing things that are wrong, you're likely to do wrong things yourself.

Sandy: That's right. They say you're a product of your environment, and I think there's something to that. When you're at an age where your values aren't settled yet, what goes on around you influences you a lot.

How do you see family life affecting the young people around you?

Carol: One of the biggest shocks I had when I went away to college was meeting friends who had four parents, or one parent, or who had a father who lived in New York and a mother that lived in California, or something like that. Or kids who just had no family structure at all. They were constantly looking for something to hang onto. It was very depressing for me because I come from a very close-knit family.

Are there other problems that the young people you know at school have to deal with?

Joe: Lots of them. Sex. Homosexuality. I know kids in high school who struggle with that. Drugs. Drinking—That's maybe the biggest one I see, even more than drugs. I know kids in college whom I would have to say are alcoholics. Perhaps their parents dealt with life by drinking, so that's the way they deal with their problems.

We always hear so much about drugs, but you think alcohol is the bigger problem?

Sandy: Ten years or so ago, I think drugs were really the big thing. But now it's alcohol. You don't see people walking down the street smoking marijuana, but you do see people sitting around drinking wine and beer. It's much easier to get, for one thing. And children often grow up seeing their parents drink, so it seems more acceptable. You don't get in as much trouble for it, but you still get high on it, which is what I think kids are looking for. It's an escape from reality.

Do your friends try to pressure you into drinking?

Mark: All the time. Friday night comes around and my friends start saying, "We're going to go hit the bars. Are you coming?" They can get real pushy. "What else are you going to do? What do you have to do that's better than hitting the bars with us?"

How do you handle that?

Mark: The main thing is to remember that I'm a Christian and I'm going to be faithful to Jesus. Sometimes I just explain it that way. If our youth group is meeting, I can just say I'm going to my youth group. Sometimes I just say, "Well, I'm going to stay home and study."

Carol: I personally don't see anything wrong with drinking, as long as it's not excessive or done just for the sake of getting high and escaping life. So sometimes I'll go along just for the fellowship, but not to get drunk. People see that and come to respect it. It's a good witness. I've been at parties where everyone was drinking and I didn't want to be part of it, so I just asked for a Coke. Sometimes people look at you funny, but usually it's no big deal.

Let's shift gears now. Instead of talking just about problems, let's talk about your relationship with God. How has your discovery of the Lord Jesus Christ influenced the way you find your identity, the way you relate to others, the way you handle challenges and difficulties?

Joe: The main thing I've found is that my relationship with the Lord gives me a basis on which to make decisions, and choices. I have something I can turn to. The Scriptures give me wisdom to make the day-to-day choices I struggle with. Instead of just turning to my environment or being shaped by the people around me, I have a place to go to find the answers to the questions everybody is asking.

So people who don't have a relationship with Jesus, or have access to his wisdom have nowhere to go to. But for you, knowing Jesus gives you a foundation. Do the rest of you have that same experience?

Sandy: I've found that a relationship with Jesus gives you a solid self-image. You can deal with yourself better. Some of my friends at school have major problems, and they have no one to turn to. They're so lost. But when I have problems, I do have someone to turn to, and my friends can see that. Sometimes when they're in trouble, they turn to me because they know I can turn to Jesus.

Are you ever ridiculed or persecuted for following Jesus?

Joe: A lot of people at school would make fun of me because they knew the reason I wasn't going out partying Saturday night was that I was planning to get up and go to church Sunday morning. They'd give me a hard time about being "Holy Joe." I'd come in from church and they'd just be getting out of bed. "Here comes Holy Joe," they'd say. "We're going to be pagans this morning." Things like that.

How did you react to that sort of thing?

Joe: It didn't really bother me that much. I just pushed it aside. I actually think several of them were searching. They'd make fun of me in front of other people, and then come up and ask, "What church do you go to? Can I go with you next week?"

So you were actually being a good witness to them even when they made fun of you. Has anyone else had other experiences?

Carol: The girls on my hall at school were very close, and most of them were good Christians. That was great. Whenever any of us had a problem, we could always find someone to talk to. Often, when you have a problem, you get upset and you can't see things clearly. But your friends can help you sort things out. They can pray with you and help you figure out what God wants you to do in the situation.

Do Christian young people have the same struggles that other young people have?

Mark: We have more struggles. We daily have to rededicate our lives to Christ. We have to decide what is right in this or that situation, when other kids don't care about what's right.

Do you ever envy them?

Mark: I never have, because they don't seem as happy. I'd rather be happy and have to struggle every day than just float through life with no goals and no reason to live.

You do seem happy. There's obviously something going on inside you that I don't always see in the lives of other young people. But you say there are still struggles. Just because you know the Lord Jesus, doesn't mean that everything's rosy.

Sandy: Right. Some days are great, but other days are hard. But it's neat when you walk across campus, and you can tell Jesus is with you. You know you're not alone. You have a friend there with you. It makes a difference, it really does.

If you could only tell other young people one thing, what would it be? What would be the one thing you'd want to get across to them?

Joe: I'd tell them not to fool themselves. Many of my friends think they know it all and have it all together. They don't need God. They don't need to pray or read the Bible, because they've got it all figured out. But they're just fooling themselves. They don't realize they can't do anything without God. They have to put God first or they don't have anything together.

Carol: I'd tell them to give Jesus a chance. Often people aren't even willing to give Jesus a chance. If they would, they'd discover that he's really offering them something good.

Clearly, Jesus Christ makes a difference, not just in a vague, "spiritual" way, but in the very down-to-earth details of living life day by day.

What I find sobering about these comments is that they indicate some very big and very widespread problems among young people today. Wherever I go, whoever I talk to, I hear the same areas mentioned: self-identity, sexuality, drugs and drinking, relationships with parents, the need for peer support. The young people quoted from in this chapter have to deal with these problems head-on as part of their daily life. So, I suspect, do most of you.

Part of the good news of Christianity, however, is that Jesus helps us deal with problems like these. The joy and strength that he imparts to us just by dwelling inside us are a big help. Moreover, he gives us wisdom—through his word in Scripture, through his Holy Spirit guiding and directing us—on which to base our lives, with which to answer the many questions that confront us. Let's consider a few of these major problem areas, and see what wisdom God has provided for us in dealing with them.

FOUR

Answers to the Tough Questions

I N THE LAST CHAPTER four young people spoke candidly about some of the challenges they face in trying to follow Jesus in their daily lives. I know from my own experience as a teacher, counselor, and youth minister that many other challenges face young people in our society. While every individual is unique, and every individual problem is likewise unique, I have noticed some recurring themes in the questions I have been asked over the years. In this chapter I'd like to share some of these questions with you, and give you my answers to them.

My parents are always telling me what to do and how to live my life. Why do I have to listen to them?

We all know the commandment, "Honor your father and mother." This is a teaching that God repeats many times, in many ways, throughout the Bible. One of my favorite expressions of it is found in the Old Testament book of Sirach:

> Children, pay heed to your father's right; do so that you may live. For the Lord sets a father in honor over his children; a mother's authority he confirms over her sons. He who honors his father atones for sins; he stores up riches who reveres his mother. He who honors his father is gladdened by children, and when he prays he is heard. He

who reveres his father will live a long life; he obeys the Lord
who brings comfort to his mother. (Sir 3:1-6)

And in the New Testament we read, "Children, obey your
parents in the Lord, for that is what is expected of you. 'Honor
your father and mother' is the first commandment to carry a
promise with it—'that it may go well with you, and that you
may have long life on the earth'" (Eph 6:1-3).

It is clearly important to God that children love, honor, and
obey their parents. It is one of the principles he has built into
the way of life he calls his people to live.

I know how strongly you desire independence. You want to
live your own life, to be your own boss, and to get "out from
under" the authority of your parents and of others God has
placed over you. But God wants you to heed the word given us
in the first Letter of Peter: "You younger men [and women]
must be obedient to your elders. . . . Clothe yourselves with
humility, because God 'is stern with the arrogant but to the
humble he shows kindness'" (1 Pt 5:5).

**That's fine if you have good, loving parents, but my
parents treat me unfairly. They're not even Christians.**

I know how difficult this kind of situation can be. But note
that Scripture does *not* say, "Honor and obey your parents as
long as they are committed Christians," or, "as long as their
directions seem wise and fair."

Bear in mind, first of all, that one of the best ways to change
the tone of any difficult relationship is to change how *we*
participate in that relationship. This is just as true of our
relationship with our parents as with anyone else. Your parents
may not be following the Lord, but you are. They may not
understand the biblical principles for conducting relationships successfully, but you do. They may not know how God
wants parents to relate to their children, but you know how
God wants children to relate to their parents.

Take the initiative yourself and let them see the change in you. Show how the grace of God has affected you and clean up your own act first. Demonstrate the love of God that has come into your heart by loving your parents.

How do you do that? You do it first of all by serving them in concrete, practical ways: help cheerfully with the chores, clean up your room without being nagged, put some gas in the car every once in a while. Second, tell your parents you love them. Have you ever tried that? I'm continually amazed and saddened by the number of young people who never tell their parents they love them. This is most important precisely when our parents seem hardest to love: it puts our heart in the right place and helps to melt their hearts so they can experience the love of God flowing through us.

Don't wait for your parents to change before you will. Make every effort to live out the wisdom of God, the teaching of Scripture, and you'll be working with God to create a new environment in your family.

Your parents are human beings. They have weaknesses. They sin. Sometimes they may hurt you by their words or actions. Sometimes you may feel like giving up—perhaps you've done your best and it doesn't seem to have worked out for the good.

But God doesn't want you to give up. He wants you to learn to accept your mother and father for who they are, and to work at being a source of joy to them even as you struggle with problems and with being misunderstood. God has selected your parents for you, and you for them. Even in difficult circumstances, God wants you to focus on obeying him in his call to love, honor, and obey your parents. As you do, he'll help you by the power of his Spirit.

What's wrong with rock music? Our parents had their own style of music when they were young. Why not us?

First of all, let's remember that God doesn't dislike music. He created music! He designed it to play an important role in our lives as human beings and as Christians. Paul encourages us to address one another "in psalms and hymns and inspired songs," and to "sing praise to the Lord with all our hearts" (see Eph 5:19).

Music has a powerful effect on us. But that effect can be either good or bad. Music can lead us closer to God, or it can lead us away from him. We need to evaluate all music on this basis: does my involvement with it lead me closer to Jesus or away from him?

With much contemporary music, it's not hard to tell what the spiritual effects are likely to be. We should have nothing to do with music that glorifies sin, rebellion, sexual immorality, suicide, drug or alcohol abuse, or that glorifies Satan and the occult.

Sometimes we say, "Yes, I know the words are bad, but I don't really pay any attention to the words. I just listen to the music." But it is a fact that our subconscious actually does retain what we hear, whether we're actively listening to it or not. We should be careful, then, about the kind of messages we let seep into our minds through the music we listen to.

It's also important to examine the lives of those who write and record the music we listen to. Musicians and recording stars easily become heroes to us. Yet many of them are living anything but holy lives, and some are openly satanic. The teaching of Jesus applies here: "Do you ever pick grapes from thornbushes, or figs from prickly plants? Never! Any sound tree bears good fruit, while a decayed tree bears bad fruit. A sound tree cannot bear bad fruit any more than a decayed tree can bear good fruit" (Mt 7:16-18). How can any music of genuine and lasting value come to us from people whose lives are radically out of God's order?

Of course, a lot of music isn't obviously sinful in these ways, but we still need to heed the scriptural warning to "test all things; reject what is evil, hold on to what is good." I think a good "test" is provided in Paul's letter to the Philippians, where he tells us that our "thoughts should be wholly directed to all that is true, all that deserves respect, all that is honest, pure, admirable, decent, virtuous, or worthy of praise" (Phil 4:8). Again, the question is simple: does listening to this music lead us closer to Jesus? If not, of what use is it to us, who have committed our lives to love and serve him?

Finally, rather than just be critical of the harmful music that the world offers us, let's take hold of the good, inspiring, Christian music that's also available to us: music that brings us joy, that refreshes us, that builds us up, that lifts our minds and hearts to love and worship our Lord.

I might mention that these principles apply not only to music, but also to movies, television, books, and magazines. These things, too, clamor for our attention and try to fill our minds with their messages. We need to be equally vigilant and discerning with them in what we allow into our minds and hearts.

I know that hard drugs like heroin and cocaine are dangerous, but what's wrong with marijuana? It's no worse than alcohol.

One of the most damaging lies going around today is the one that says that marijuana is not harmful. That is simply not true. It *is* harmful. From my pastoral experience, I know the subtle deterioration that takes place in the minds and personalities of people who use drugs, including pot. It may not always be measurable in the chemical tests that the scientists run, but it is there just the same.

Often, when a young person gets into using marijuana, he or she does it to avoid coping with life, to set up a screen that filters out the unpleasant realities of life. But God's will for us is to learn to overcome those difficulties with his power, not to hide from them. His will is to use those challenges to strengthen us and to develop our faith and character. When we cop out on life by using drugs, we short-circuit God's plan and rob ourselves of the opportunity to grow. Instead of becoming stronger individuals, we become weaker.

Besides, the filtering screen we set up blocks out more than just the hassles of life. It also blocks out the full, free operation of the Holy Spirit. It makes it that much more difficult for the power of a loving, healing, saving, caring God to get through to us.

Nor does God want us to surrender control over our minds and spirits to drugs. In his letter to the Galatians, Paul says that one fruit of the Spirit is self-control (Gal 5:23). Peter urges us to always stay "sober and alert" so that we can deal with the spiritual warfare that surrounds us in the power of God (1 Pt 5:8). We need to be in control of our faculties so we can be sensitive to what God is doing in and through us. We can't do that when we're high on drugs.

Only Jesus can ultimately help us overcome the problems we encounter. He alone can give us the inner strength to cope with any situation, any hurt, any trial, any disappointment, any alienation, any loneliness. Getting high isn't the answer to our problems. Jesus is. God does not want us to look for artificial, chemically induced highs, but instead to seek after the lasting joy and true inner peace that come only from him.

What about alcohol? I think people are being hypocritical when they tell young people that drinking is wrong. Society obviously thinks it's okay.

The Bible does not teach us that the use of alcohol is automatically wrong in and of itself, but it does teach us that the abuse of alcohol is wrong. And our experience certainly shows us how common this abuse is in our culture. Addiction to alcohol is frighteningly common. How many individual lives have been destroyed by alcohol! How many marriages have been ruined by alcohol and families torn apart by it! How much child abuse and spouse abuse can be traced to it!

While there is an appropriate use of alcohol, Scripture nevertheless warns us repeatedly not to become intoxicated.

"Avoid getting drunk on wine," Paul tells the Ephesians, because it "leads to debauchery." Instead, he says, "Be filled with the Spirit" (Eph 5:18). My comments earlier regarding drugs—not using them to escape from our problems, not surrendering control of our minds and wills—also apply to drinking.

Peer pressure to use drugs and to abuse alcohol can be severe. And I recognize that society's acceptance of drinking, and its increasing acceptance of drugs, make this pressure even more difficult to withstand. But surely, witnessing the tragedy and heartache that people in our society experience because of alcohol and drug abuse should warn us not to follow their example. God wants us to stand apart from the crowd, from those who are lost in the darkness of not knowing him. He wants us to shine like lights in the midst of their darkness and show them the way to himself.

Sometimes my friends and I like to read our horoscopes in the newspaper or talk about our zodiac sign and what it means. Some people say this is wrong. Why? It seems like harmless fun to me.

Nowadays, you can hardly open a newspaper or go to the supermarket without running into horoscopes, signs of the zodiac, or other expressions of the occult. Most people consider these as innocent or amusing pastimes. But Scripture clearly indicates that all occult signs or symbols are rooted in religious systems that lead us away from God and into the spiritual realm controlled by the evil one. Whether we intend it or not, whether we realize it or not, involvement with the occult is spiritually dangerous. This is true of horoscopes and the signs of the zodiac, seances, Ouija boards, psychic experiences, and any other activities with occult or spiritist overtones.

Most of these activities stem from the normal human desire to understand the future, to seek guidance about what we should do. But the Lord warns us not to surrender control of our consciousness to anyone or anything but his Holy Spirit, and not to seek guidance for our lives from anyone but himself, his word, and the teaching of his church. The only "sign" a Christian should live under is the sign of the cross!

If you've been involved in astrology, in contacting spirits, or in any such activity, clearly and verbally renounce your involvement in the occult, resolve to have nothing more to do with it, and ask God to forgive you. Get rid of any literature or paraphernalia you may have collected that is related to the occult. Decide to make Jesus your only source of wisdom, guidance, and spiritual insight, and turn your back on anything that might lead you away from him.

I'm struggling with homosexual feelings. I know the Bible says it's wrong, but what if that's just the way I'm made? I'm confused.

Let me assure you that I understand, and the Lord understands, the struggle you're going through over your sexual identity. You needn't be ashamed of the struggle. In fact, you need to be open and honest about what you're experiencing, both with the Lord and with mature Christian men or women who can help you.

The mere fact that you experience some homosexual feelings does *not* mean you should classify yourself as a homosexual or a lesbian. Doing that will only make the feelings more difficult to deal with.

You are correct in noting that the Bible says homosexuality is wrong, but we should distinguish between homosexual feelings or temptations on the one hand, and homosexual acts on the other. Homosexual feelings and temptations are not sinful. Temptations and feelings are never sinful in and of themselves. They are merely opportunities for us to choose to do right or to do wrong.

Homosexual activity, however, is indeed wrong. It is not in

accord with God's design for human sexuality. In our day, when there is such confusion on this issue, it is necessary to state clearly that active homosexuality is a sin.

But never forget that God wants to forgive this sin just as much as he wants to forgive any other sin. And he wants to give grace to overcome this problem just as much as he wants to give grace to overcome any other problem. God can give you everything you need to live a holy and righteous life as his son or daughter. No situation is hopeless, because our hope is in Jesus Christ.

I encourage those of you who are struggling with this particular problem to seek the counsel and support of a mature Christian whose personal life is in good order and who accepts the moral teachings of Scripture. You need not fight this battle alone.

Finally, always keep in mind the words of Paul: "No test has been sent you that does not come to all men. Besides, God keeps his promise. He will not let you be tested beyond your strength. Along with the test he will give you a way out of it so that you may be able to endure it" (1 Cor 10:13).

In the next chapter let me share with you some thoughts about the whole area of personal sexuality. While not an exhaustive presentation on the subject, I hope what you read will help you move in the right direction of being "a continual example of love, faith and purity to believers" (1 Tim 4:12).

FIVE

The Other Half of the Human Race

O F ALL THE AREAS that raise questions and difficulties for young people, perhaps none is so trying as the area of sexuality.

It's not hard to see why. When it comes to this aspect of human life, we seem to live in two worlds at once. The world around us exalts sexual indulgence at every turn. Physical attractiveness is glorified; strength of character and what Scripture calls "the beauty of holiness" is ignored. Seductiveness and promiscuity are modeled for us on television, in the movies, and in popular music; modesty and chastity are ridiculed.

All these things have served to take the meaning out of sex: it's cut off from its connection to relationships of commitment and love, and is seen as just an enjoyable physical activity engaged in by "consenting adults" (or by "consenting teenagers") whenever the urge strikes. And, with the help of our society as well as our own natural instincts, the urge seems to strike almost constantly!

At the same time, God warns us not to give in to the lies of the evil one and the phony allurements of the world. Where the world tells us that sex is merely a matter of hormones, the Lord tells us that he created sex, and that sex is of immense importance to our development as spiritual beings. Where the world treats sex casually, God tells us that sex finds its proper expression only in marriage, and that indulging in it outside of marriage can only lead to pain, disorder, and sin.

And so we feel caught in an immense tug-of-war: torn between the high and hard road to genuine happiness that God and the church present to us, and the false, fleeting "happiness" into which the world tries to draw us. How do we get out of this trap?

The Way God Planned It

First, we need to understand God's plan for human sexuality.

I cannot emphasize strongly enough that our sexuality is something that God has given us, something that God looks upon as good. It's easy, when we're hearing lectures (or reading books!) about the dangers of sexual sin, to conclude that God thinks sexual desire is inherently dirty or sinful.

That's not the case. God knows the desires, the appetites, the drives within us. He himself put them there, and for an important reason.

God designed sexual intimacy to express committed love between a man and a woman. There's something so deep, so intense, so profound about sex that it really only "fits" in the context of a love relationship that's equally deep, equally intense, equally profound. There's something dynamic, something alive, something explosive about sexual intimacy that can only be fully and properly released in the context of a relationship that's stable, solid, and secure. And no such relationship can exist apart from the covenant of marriage.

Sex touches on some of the deepest parts of our nature as human beings. Our sexuality is a powerful force within us, with great potential for shaping our lives. In its proper context, it can help move us toward our greatest fulfillment as human beings. Apart from its proper context, it can become a force that drives us toward disintegration and death.

Scripture and the church teach us so forcefully about sexual sin not because God wants to deny us pleasure or personal fulfillment, but because he doesn't want us to miss the higher pleasure and the particular fulfillment that our sexuality was especially designed to bring us.

What are the main sexual sins mentioned in Scripture and church teaching? *Fornication* is sexual intimacy outside of the covenant relationship of marriage. *Adultery* is sexual intimacy apart from the particular covenant relationship to which one or the other parties is bound. *Masturbation* is the indulging of sexual desire for merely selfish pleasure. *Homosexuality* is sexual intimacy in the context of a relationship that can never fulfill God's intent.

We should see these sins, not as the use of something bad—as if sex were bad in itself—but as the inadequate or disordered use of something good. They each fall short of the glory of proper expression of human sexuality as God has designed it.

In fact, sex is so sacred in God's eyes, so holy, so powerful in its effects upon us, that he calls us not only to restrain our bodies from physically misusing it, but also to restrain our minds from misusing it. Jesus teaches us, "You have heard the commandment, 'You shall not commit adultery.' What I say to you is: anyone who looks lustfully at a woman has already committed adultery with her in his thoughts" (Mt 5:27-28).

The basic principle is simply stated: God has created human sexuality as the expression of committed love between one man and one woman, in the context of the covenant relationship of marriage. Any other use of it, no matter how pleasurable it may seem for the moment, will inevitably deprive us of the blessings God wants us to draw from it. If we live out our sexuality according to God's plan, we will experience the fruit of love, joy, and security, but if we pursue sexual pleasure apart from God's plan, we will experience the fruit of lust, guilt, and loneliness.

How Far Is Too Far?

Frequently I am asked, "How far is too far? How far can my girlfriend and I go in expressing our affection? Is kissing okay? What about other actions short of actual intercourse? Where do you draw the line between what's sinful and what's okay?"

I think asking the question this way puts things in the wrong light. We need to understand that God has made us in such a way that "one thing leads to another." The fact is that intimate kissing, necking, touching, caressing—are all *designed* to move us toward full sexual union. They're not intended to satisfy us in and of themselves. They're actually *meant* to stir up in us a desire to go further.

So what we should really ask ourselves, is: "Is it right for me to have sexual intercourse with this person at this time?" If not, then why set in motion a sequence of events whose very purpose is to take you where you should not go? If you know from the start that you cannot follow a path to its only logical destination, why set out on the journey?

The biblical book, Song of Songs, contains some wise advice on this point: "Do not arouse, do not stir up love before its own time" (Song 3:5). It's important that we not stir into flame feelings and desires that cannot rightly be satisfied.

In fact, fire is a helpful image for understanding how we need to handle our sexual desire. Fire, as we all know, is a good thing and has many important uses: it's a source of energy, and it provides light and warmth. But we also know that fire can be harmful—it can burn and destroy. Fire is good, but it needs to be used under the proper conditions. It needs to be kept in the fireplace.

So it is with sex. Sex is good, but it needs to be used under the proper conditions. It needs to be kept in the "fireplace" that God has designed for it: Christian marriage. Otherwise, it can burn out of control and hurt us.

The Price We Pay

What are some of the dangers of allowing this fire to burn outside the fireplace? How can sex hurt us if we engage in it outside of God's plan?

1. It tears down our relationship with God. The simple fact is that sexual activity outside of marriage is sin, and like all sin it opens a gulf between us and God. It says to God that we do not choose to obey him, to live as he has taught us. Once we have tasted the peace and joy that comes from living in a love relationship with God, why would we want to do anything to harm that relationship?

2. It brings us under a burden of guilt. In spite of all the arguments for why sex outside of marriage is okay, and in spite of all the ways we try to justify it to ourselves, something inside us knows it's wrong. Wrong sexual activity inevitably leads to feelings of guilt that rob us of our own peace of mind, make us feel distant from God, and even undermine the very relationship we tried to strengthen through sex.

3. It leads to unwanted pregnancy. Obviously, one of the main purposes of sexual intercourse is procreation—having children. Yet an amazing number of people overlook, or deliberately refuse to recognize, this possibility. The incidence of pregnancy among young people is alarming, and it's rising. This in turn brings the problems and heartache of young people trying to raise a child before they are ready for it—or to the temptation to get an abortion and kill the new life God has created. Abortion is a serious sin forbidden by God and the church. The Catholic Church excommunicates anyone who procures an abortion, so serious a violation of God's law is this crime.

Many young people fool themselves in this area by saying, "It won't happen to me." But sadly, it often does. Until we are ready to take on the responsibilities of parenthood, we simply have no business getting involved in sexual intercourse, nor in any physical activity that leads to intercourse.

4. We risk getting venereal disease. Doctors say our society is in the midst of an epidemic of sexually transmitted disease. We have all heard the stories of those who suffer from AIDS, herpes, and other diseases. This occurs among young people no less than among others. Venereal disease is one of the tragic consequences of sexual activity apart from God's plan, and it can have an enormous impact on a person's ability to enter into marriage later in life.

5. It devalues sex in marriage. We are told by our society that unless we experiment widely with sex while we are single, we won't be able to adjust to sex when we get married. Nothing could be further from the truth. There really is something special, something precious, about entering into marriage knowing that we have saved ourselves for the one special person God has provided for us as a life partner.

At the risk of sounding old-fashioned, let me say our virginity is among the greatest gifts we can give to our future husband or wife—and this is true for men as well as for women. To surrender our virginity before marriage is to cheat ourselves of one the greatest blessings God wants to give us. Respect for chastity, purity and virginity are values God wants to restore to our society. Among members of the Body of Christ these values should be held in high esteem.

Holiness and Happiness

For those of us who are followers of Jesus, the path of righteousness and holiness is clearly laid out for us in Scripture.

"As obedient sons [and daughters], do not yield to the desires that once shaped you in your ignorance," Peter writes. "Rather, become holy yourselves in every aspect of your conduct, after the likeness of the Holy One who called you; remember, Scripture says, 'Be holy, for I am holy'" (1 Pt 1:14-16).

The idea that holiness and happiness can't go together is a lie, and we don't have to be deceived by it. God's call to us to be holy with regard to our sexuality is not meant to rob us of joy. Rather, it's meant to lead us to even greater joy. "Your hearts will rejoice," Jesus promises us, "with a joy no one can take from you" (Jn 16:22).

Nor is God's call to purity meant to deprive us of supportive and life-giving relationships with members of the opposite sex. Quite the opposite! It is precisely as we learn to relate to one another with honest, generous, self-sacrificing love—without all the game-playing and selfishness that so often go with the "love" based on mere sexual attraction—that we will experience the most fulfilling, the most satisfying, the most up-building relationships with members of the opposite sex. We will relate to each other not merely as objects of sexual desire, but as true brothers and sisters in the Lord.

This is the point of Paul's advice to Timothy: "You should treat younger men as brothers, older women as mothers, and younger women as sisters, with absolute purity" (1 Tm 5:1-2).

The Dating Game

What about dating? Is dating appropriate?

"Dating" as we know it was unknown in Bible times, so Scripture doesn't address it directly. For this reason, I offer my perspective not as a direct teaching from the Lord but as my discernment of what is wise and appropriate.

My best judgment is that serious dating, or courtship, is appropriate only in the context of setting out toward marriage. I believe that for young people who are not yet ready for marriage to get involved in intense, exclusive guy-girl relationships—which is almost always the result, if not the object, of dating—is inappropriate. It draws us into a world of emotional entanglements and heartaches that we're not prepared for, and it cuts us off from healthy peer relationships with the broader group of our brothers and sisters. It frequently leads to overpowering sexual temptation.

I think most young people use dating as a way of meeting genuine needs that they have: needs for personal confidence, for acceptance by others, for social activity. I believe the Lord wants these needs to be met through our relationship with him and our peer relationships with brothers and sisters in Christ, not through exclusive guy-girl relationships.

The Assurance of Forgiveness

Perhaps you have stumbled in one of the areas covered in these last two chapters. You may now have realized ways in which you have fallen short of the standard of holiness he calls us to.

Perhaps you acted in ignorance: you simply didn't know God's plan. Perhaps you did know what was the right thing to do, but gave in to peer pressure. Or perhaps you willfully did wrong: you knew what you should have done, but you gave in to the inclination toward sin that dwells within each of us.

Whatever the case may be, I assure you that there's no sin so big, so black, so burdensome, that it cannot be washed away in the blood of Jesus Christ. His love is stronger than our rebellion, and his forgiveness is bigger than our sin. There's no sin that Jesus can't wash away, no hurt that he can't heal, no scar that he can't remove, if only we turn to him in repentance, confess our sin, and ask him to help us follow God's ways more faithfully in the future.

Prayer of Commitment

Jesus, I love you.
I am sorry for my sins.
I thank you for dying on the cross for me personally.
I celebrate your Resurrection this beautiful day by giving my life to you.

I invite you into my life, into my home, into my business, into my school, into my recreation, into wherever I am.

Come, Lord Jesus.
I truly accept you as my Lord and God and my personal Savior.
Come now and fill me with your Spirit;
Fill me Lord Jesus with your Holy Spirit.
Fill me Lord Jesus with your love and send me forth to my family and friends, to be able to share with them your love and your concern.
Jesus, I love you and I shall follow you as your disciple every day of my life.
Amen.

SIX

Seven Ingredients of Joy

MANY PEOPLE THINK of the Christian life as a grim, drab, joyless experience. Jesus, however, promises us just the opposite. He says that our relationship with him will give us "a joy that no one can take from us" (see John 16:22).

Joy. It's a word we've all heard a lot. The Bible speaks of it often. But what does it mean? And how do we get it? That's what this chapter is about.

One of the clearest explanations of Christian joy comes from Jesus himself: "All this I tell you that my joy may be yours and your joy may be complete" (Jn 15:11). This verse tells us two very important things about joy:

That my joy may be yours. First, the joy we are looking for in our lives comes from Jesus. It's *his* joy we are to experience. He gives it to us and as we shall see, he gives it to us by his Holy Spirit.

That your joy may be complete. Second, Jesus wants us to let his joy fill us to overflowing. He wants our lives to be totally and completely filled with the joy that comes from him.

Most of us, when we think of the word joy, think of the way we feel when we're having a really great day or when something terrific has happened to us. It's a kind of emotional high. Is that what Jesus is talking about here? Are we supposed to go around feeling giddy all the time?

There's a lot more to it than that. When we know and love

57

and live for Jesus, we *do* experience it in our emotions. Those kinds of feelings do come. But joy is deeper than that. It's the strong, steady awareness that we are loved, that we are cared for, that our heavenly Father and our elder Brother are watching out for us, that the Holy Spirit is living deep inside us. As this strong, steady awareness takes hold of us, it produces in us an abiding sense of joy that we experience whether or not we're breaking out in goose bumps at the moment.

Joy stands, first of all, for "*Jesus Over You.*" There is no joy apart from Jesus. Remember, the joy we're after is *his* joy. It can only come from him. If we're going to know true joy, we have to let Jesus be in charge of our life.

Joy stands, secondly, for "*Jesus—Others—You.*" There are priorities in our lives. First comes Jesus and our relationship with him. Then, out of that relationship flows our love and service to others around us. And finally, as we live in Jesus and give ourselves to the service of others, we find our own true identity. To know Jesus' joy, we have to arrange our lives according to Jesus' priorities. When our priorities get out of order, we can't have the joy he wants us to have.

This gives us a clearer picture of what joy *is*. It's the abiding awareness of God's love for us. It's the security of being submitted to Jesus' lordship. It's having our lives in order according to Jesus' priorities. But how do we *get* joy? I would like to list seven ingredients of joy—seven aspects of the "Jesus Over You" relationship.

1. Recognize Your Unique Value in God's Eyes

"I have called you by name, you are mine" (Is 43:1, RSV). This verse speaks of the Lord's intimate, personal knowledge of each of us, and of the special relationship he wants to have with each of us.

The Lord wants you to know that you are unique. There is

no other person in all the world exactly like you. There never has been, and there never will be. That makes you special to God. He has given you a unique personality, a unique destiny, a unique calling in life.

"Before I formed you in the womb I knew you, and before you were born I consecrated you; I appointed you a prophet to the nations" (Jer 1:5, RSV). God's words to Jeremiah apply to you as well. He knew you even before you were born, and he chose you to be his son, his daughter, his servant. He wants to have a once-in-all-eternity relationship with you. What joy comes simply from realizing that God knows you, has called you by name, and wants to share a special relationship with you!

2. Receive God's Forgiveness

Someone has said that every man and woman has a "God-shaped hole" in his heart, an emptiness that only God himself can fill. As we well know, many people around us experience that emptiness. They try to fill it in many ways: with drugs, alcohol, sexual promiscuity, and many other things. But the only thing that can fill our emptiness is the abiding presence of God in our hearts.

We all have our struggles, but Jesus can give us victory over them. When we live our life in the Lord, loving him, walking with him, surrendering ourselves to him, he frees us from all those things that claim to satisfy our inner emptiness but can never do it.

Jesus can also free us from our guilt. When we sin, we cut ourselves off from the joy God wants for us, and instead we experience guilt. But God has given us the cure for guilt. That cure is the forgiveness of our sins through the blood of Jesus.

The apostle John makes this very clear. He says, "The blood of his Son Jesus cleanses us from all sin" (1 Jn 1:7). Not just from *some* sins, mind you, but from *all* sin. How do we receive this cleansing? "If we acknowledge our sins, he who is just can be trusted to forgive our sins and cleanse us from every wrong" (1 Jn 1:9).

We hear many people talk about liberation these days. But Jesus Christ is the true liberator. He sets us free from the guilt brought on by our sin. All we need to do is "acknowledge" our sins—confess them to the Lord—and he promises to cleanse us from *every* wrong.

Any time your daily walk with the Lord is interrupted by sin, any time you experience guilt crowding out joy in your heart, acknowledge your sins to God and receive his forgiveness. Don't hang on to your sin and guilt. Release it to Jesus. When we get off our chest all the things that weigh us down with guilt, we can walk on, knowing that we are cleansed and purified, and restored to fellowship with Jesus.

3. Become Jesus' Disciple

"Live on in me, as I do in you. No more than a branch can bear fruit of itself apart from the vine, can you bear fruit apart from me. I am the vine, you are the branches. He who lives in me and I in him, will produce abundantly, for apart from me you can do nothing" (Jn 15:4-5).

Jesus himself speaks to us in this passage, and he tells us we must dedicate ourselves to "living on" in him. Some translations here say "abide" in him or "continue" in him. However we translate it, the meaning is clear: our relationship with Jesus is not to be just a one-time or occasional experience. It is supposed to be consistent, lasting, steady. We are to remain united to him on a day-to-day basis.

This "living on" in Jesus is what we call discipleship. We are called to be *disciples* of Jesus, not just fans or admirers of him. A disciple lives with his master. He walks and talks with his master day by day. Most of all, a disciple seeks to be shaped into the image and likeness of his master.

4. Be Molded by the Master Potter

"O Lord, thou art our Father; we are the clay, and thou art our potter; we are all the work of thy hand" (Is 64:8, RSV). True joy comes when we place ourselves in Jesus' hands like clay in the hands of a potter, when we let him shape and mold our minds, our hearts, our emotions, our values, our attitudes, our behavior.

How does Jesus mold us? The same way he molded the lives of the earliest Christians: through "the apostles' instructions and the communal life, to the breaking of bread and the prayer" (Acts 2:42). That is, he molds us by the Holy Spirit working through our daily times of prayer, our faithful participation in the life of the church, and through our diligent study and meditation on Scripture.

Prayer. "The Paraclete, the Holy Spirit whom the Father will send in my name, will instruct you in everything, and remind you of all that I told you" (Jn 14:26). We need our daily prayer times. We need to be alone with the Lord in a consistent way. We need to make opportunities to listen to the still, small voice of God as it is whispered in our hearts by the Holy Spirit, teaching us, correcting us, guiding us, molding us.

The Church. Speaking to the apostles, to those who were to inherit responsibility for his church, Jesus said, "He who hears you, hears me" (Lk 10:16). The Lord wants to shape and mold us through the ministry of his church, through our common worship, through the teaching of the Pope and the bishops, through our life lived together under the guidance of his Holy Spirit.

Scripture. "All Scripture is inspired of God and is useful for teaching—for reproof, correction, and training in holiness so that the man of God may be fully competent and equipped for every good work" (2 Tm 3:16). The Bible is, quite simply, God's word addressed to every one of us. It is the definitive revelation of who he is, and who we are, and how he wants us to live. We need to take the time to study God's word, to take it into our hearts and let it mold and form us.

"Anyone who hears my words and puts them into practice is like the wise man who built his house on rock. When the rainy season set in, the torrents came and the winds blew and buffeted his house. It did not collapse; it had been solidly set on rock. Anyone who hears my words but does not put them into practice is like the foolish man who built his house on sandy ground. The rains fell, the torrents came, the winds blew and lashed against his house. It collapsed under all this and was completely ruined" (Mt 7:24-27).

How do we allow the word of God to have its full effect in our lives? By putting it into practice. We are not just to listen to the words of the Lord. We are to apply them in our daily lives. God's word is not meant simply for intellectualizing—it is meant for living. What joy is there in knowing the truth but not living it? In having practical wisdom but not applying it? The joy of Jesus comes not just from *hearing* his word, but from *doing* it (see Jas 1:23-25).

Don't let your values and attitudes be formed by the world around you, by television or movies or popular music. Don't let these be the main things that you let into your life, the main things you respond to. Joy comes from being formed by the Holy Spirit into the image and likeness of Jesus Christ.

5. Live in the Power of the Holy Spirit

"In the time after his suffering he showed them in many convincing ways that he was alive, appearing to them over the course of forty days and speaking to them about the reign of God. On one occasion when he met with them, he told them not to leave Jerusalem: 'Wait, rather, for the fulfillment of my Father's promise, of which you heard me speak. John baptized with water, but within a few days you will be baptized with the Holy Spirit'" (Acts 1:3-5).

This account of Jesus' words and actions in the days between his resurrection and his ascension into heaven shows us the importance he placed on having his disciples live in the Holy Spirit. You might think that seeing the risen, glorified Jesus and hearing him speak of the kingdom of God would have been enough for the early disciples. What could bring you more joy than to see the risen Jesus with your own eyes? But Jesus tells his followers to wait. For what? For the Holy Spirit, in which he had promised to baptize them.

It's the same with us. We need the Holy Spirit. We can't live for Jesus without the Holy Spirit. We can't have Jesus' joy unless the Holy Spirit gives birth to it within our heart. Scripture says joy is part of the fruit of the Spirit (Gal 5:22). That means it only comes from the Holy Spirit dwelling inside us.

Perhaps some of you are thinking, "But don't I already have the Holy Spirit? I was baptized and I was confirmed. Doesn't that mean I have the Holy Spirit in me already?"

Yes, it does. But the important thing is that you allow the grace of baptism and confirmation to be stirred up within you. Paul told Timothy, "I remind you to *stir into flame* the gift of God bestowed when my hands were laid on you" (2 Tm 1:6). How many people get baptized and then don't live out their faith? How many get confirmed and then just shrivel up spiritually? Pray that the Lord fan into flame the gift of the Holy Spirit that has been given you. Then the Spirit can produce the fruit of joy in your life.

6. Pray with Confidence

One of the most exciting promises that the Lord makes to us again and again in Scripture is that he will always hear our prayers.

"If our consciences have nothing to charge us with, we can be sure that God is with us and that we will receive at his hands whatever we ask. Why? Because we are keeping his commandments and doing what is pleasing in his sight" (1 Jn 3:21-22).

"We have this confidence in God: that he hears us whenever

we ask for anything according to his will. And since we know that he hears us whenever we ask, we know that what we have asked him for is ours" (1 Jn 5:14-15).

"Rejoice in the Lord always! I say it again. Rejoice! Everyone should see how unselfish you are. The Lord is near. Dismiss all anxiety from your minds. Present your needs to God in every form of prayer and in petitions full of gratitude. Then God's own peace, which is beyond all understanding, will stand guard over your hearts and minds, in Christ Jesus" (Phil 4:4-7).

One of our greatest sources of joy is knowing that we have access to the throne room of God. When we ask God to listen to us, he does. And he listens to us in love, wanting what is best for us, wanting to teach us what to ask for, wanting to give us the things we do ask for.

When we're struggling with some personal problem and feeling torn up inside, it's a great joy to remember that Jesus understands exactly what we're going through, and that when we cry out to him he'll give us what we need to cope with our circumstances. Likewise, when we're concerned about some serious problem in the world around us, it's a great joy to know that we're not powerless in the face of it. As our hearts and minds are conformed to God's will, we can pray to God about world problems and know that we, weak and tiny as we are, are making a difference. As James reminds us, "The fervent petition of a holy man is powerful indeed" (Jas 5:16). Jesus put it even more explicitly: "I give you my assurance, whatever you ask the Father, he will give you in my name. . . . Ask and you shall receive, that your joy may be full" (Jn 16:23-24).

7. Love One Another

"This is my commandment: love one another as I have loved you" (Jn 15:12).

This is surely one of the most powerful and most challenging lines in all of Scripture. Note that Jesus does not say, "This is my suggestion." He does not say, "This is my recommendation." He does not say, "Here's a pointer that I think will help you out." He says, "This is my *commandment*: love one another."

And he goes on to spell out just what kind of love he's talking about. He's not talking about the kind of love you see in the movies or on the soap operas. He's talking about the kind of love he showed when he stretched out his arms on the cross and gave his life. "Love one another *as I have loved you*."

The witness that is given to the world when Christians love one another this way is enormous. Jesus said, "This is how all will know you for my disciples: your love for one another" (Jn 13:35).

Love one another. Care for one another. Affirm one another. Speak well of one another. Avoid negative humor—humor at the expense of someone else. Avoid sarcasm. Avoid "put-downs."

When you wake up each morning, say to yourself, "Because I'm a follower of Jesus Christ, branded with the sign of the cross, I'm going to be a person who speaks love, affirmation, and praise. I'm going to build others up, not tear them down. In this cold, impersonal world, I'm going to dare to be different. I'm going to be someone who loves."

There is tremendous power in this kind of love. There is unspeakable joy in loving others, and in being loved by others, with this kind of love.

These, then, are the seven ingredients of joy:
—Recognize your uniqueness
—Receive God's forgiveness
—Become Jesus' disciple
—Be molded by the master potter
—Live in the power of the Holy Spirit

—Pray with confidence
—Love one another

These are seven ways to put "Jesus Over You," seven ways to live out the priorities of "Jesus-Others-Yourself." See for yourself whether following this seven-part recipe for living doesn't bring forth joy in your life!

SEVEN

On Fire for Jesus

I DON'T KNOW HOW MANY TIMES I have read in a newspaper or magazine, or heard on a radio or television program, that the age of heroes is dead. Young people today have no one to look up to, it is said; no one to model themselves after.

I'm not so sure. For one thing, I think young people have lots of people—rock musicians, athletes, movie stars, political figures—whom they model themselves after.

Who Are Your Heroes?

Who are *your* heroes? You may not think you have any, but the odds are you do. Who are they?

It's not hard to find out. Whose posters do you have hanging on your wall? Whose pictures do you have taped inside your locker at school? Who do you like to read about? Whose photograph on the cover of a magazine makes you want to buy that magazine? Whose movies do you rush to see when they first come out? Whose records do you buy when they're first released?

Whether you've ever thought about those people as "heroes" or not, they are in fact the people you're looking up to, the people you're modeling yourself after to some degree.

That's the first reason why I say the age of heroes isn't dead. There seem to be plenty of "heroes" around.

The Ultimate Hero

But there is another reason why I say that the age of heroes isn't dead. That's because there is one person who *does* deserve to be looked up to, who *is* worth modeling ourselves after. There is one person who is rightly the true hero of the human race: our Lord Jesus Christ.

Place no one in your life ahead of the Lord Jesus. No rock singer. No television personality. No movie star. No athlete. No politician. No preacher. Let no one be first in your life other than Jesus Christ. Let him be your hero.

That's not just my good advice, either. That's the way the Lord himself wants it to be. It is he who says to us, "Come to me. Let me be your hero. Let me be first in your life." Why does he insist on this? Because he knows that we cannot fulfill our potential as human beings, or be all we are meant to be, unless we are heart and soul, mind and strength, top to bottom, head over heels, committed to him in love.

Living at Full Throttle

There really is no other way. Christianity is like a car that only runs when the gas pedal is pressed to the floor. It just doesn't work at any level less than total commitment. Jesus doesn't want us to be wishy-washy, namby-pamby, on-again-off-again, lukewarm Christians. He wants us to be hard core, all-out, full-time, full-tilt, full-speed-ahead *disciples*. He wants us to be on fire for him.

Does that sound a little extreme? It's not. In fact, it's perfectly normal. It's normal to live all-out for Jesus. It's normal to love him with all your mind, heart, soul, and strength. It's normal to study the Bible and do what it says. It's normal to be filled with the power of the Holy Spirit and exercise spiritual gifts. It's normal to go to prayer meetings and sing and shout and raise your hands in praise. It's the people who *don't* know Jesus and who *aren't* living all-out for him who aren't normal!

And don't let yourself think that you're less of a man, or less of a woman, if you live for Jesus. I've got news for you. You become less of a man, and less of a woman, to the extent that you *don't* walk in the power of his Spirit.

The Love That's Tough

I need to be careful here not to make loving the Lord sound like just a matter of feelings. A lot of times when people say, "I love the Lord," what they mean is, "I feel excited about the Lord."

Now it's fine to have affectionate feelings about the Lord. But love is more than just a feeling. It's a decision. There will be times in your life when those "good feelings" about the Lord won't be there. That's when you need to be able to say, "I love you, Lord, whether I feel it or not."

Scriptural love isn't just a matter of the emotions. It's a matter of the mind and will and heart. It's not just goose-bumps—something on the surface—but it flows from the very core of our being, the place where God's Spirit dwells within us. It's the kind of love that's tough, the kind that hangs in there when times are hard and the heat is on. It's the kind of love that sticks with prayer, and sticks with Scripture study, and sticks with service to others, even when you "don't feel like it right now." That kind of love is an unquenchable flame within us that enables us to always be on fire for the Lord.

On Fire for Jesus

The normal condition of every man and woman is to be *on fire for Jesus*. That's what he wants for us. That's what he gives us the power for when he gives us his Holy Spirit.

I'm particularly fond of the word "fire" as a way to sum up

what our life in the Lord is supposed to look like. In fact, once a month I speak about it at major rallies in cities around the world as part of a ministry called "FIRE." The four letters that make up our name stand for four important ingredients of a life lived all-out for Jesus. Let me share with you four simple points that will help you live your life "on fire for Jesus."

F stands for *Faith*. Faith isn't just a matter of the intellect. It isn't just a matter of saying, "I know the answers to all the catechism questions." It includes the intellect, but it's a lot deeper than that.

Faith has to do with a personal relationship. It has to do with an intimate love relationship with the living God. It means knowing Jesus Christ personally—not just knowing things *about* him, but actually knowing *him*. It means walking with him daily in prayer and Scripture and Christian fellowship. Faith isn't a way of thinking, it's a way of living.

I stands for *Intercession*. Intercession flows naturally out of our faith, out of our intimate relationship with God. When we know God personally and are dwelling continually in his presence, it's the most natural thing in the world for us to talk with him about our family and friends, and to ask him to help them.

To intercede means to "stand in the gap" for someone else, to come before the Lord on their behalf. I'm sure you know people who need God in their lives, who need his wisdom, his power, his comfort. Well, you can help them get the help they need by interceding for them before God. As you do, you'll experience your own relationship with the Lord growing stronger and more alive.

R stands for *Repentance*. I know that to many of us, the word "repentance" has an unpleasant ring to it. We don't like to think about repenting, because we don't like to think about sin—especially about our own sin.

But repentance is actually a joyful thing. Our repentance not only brings great joy to the Lord (see Lk 15:7), but it adds to our own joy as well. It's not hard to see why. To sin means "to miss the mark," to go off course in our pursuit of God's life. Once we've recognized how good it is to live God's life and have made up our minds to pursue it with all our hearts, then when the Holy Spirit points out to us some way in which we've gone off course, we're glad to find out about it. The faster we discover how we've veered off course, the faster we can get back on track. Our response should be not, "Oh no, I've sinned, and now I have to repent," but, "Praise God, I see now where I went wrong, and now I can repent!" Availing ourselves of the Sacrament of Reconciliation is an excellent way of entering into this joy.

"Daily repentance" doesn't mean "daily self-condemnation and guilt." It just means seeking the Lord regularly for any "course corrections" we might need to make so we can stay firmly planted in his will for our lives.

E stands for *Evangelism.* I am going to look at this topic a little more closely than the others, because it is such a crucial one. It is one of the areas where the Lord needs young people most. That's right, where the Lord *needs* you. Do you realize how important you are to the advancement of God's plan? Jesus is interested in you not just for your own sake—although that's certainly part of it—but also for his sake, and for the sake of those who still need to hear about him.

All around the world there are millions of people your age who need to hear about Jesus Christ. There are young people caught up in drugs, alcohol, sexual activity, abortion, rebellion, loneliness, alienation, and despair. There are young people who are in just the same condition as my friend Douglas, the young man whose story I told in the opening chapter of this book.

Some of these young people live next door to you. Some of them are in your classes at school, or on your sports team. Some of them may even be living under the same roof as you:

your own brothers and sisters, members of your family.

God wants to reach them. He wants to free them from their sin and weakness and despair. He wants to give them life, and hope, and a future filled with the joy of loving him. He wants to give them the same things he's given you.

He also knows that it's primarily through you that he's going to be able to reach them. The best evangelizers of the young are the young. Who is going to be better able to reach the young men and women that you regularly come into contact with than you yourself?

The Catholic Church clearly recognizes this. The Second Vatican Council, in its *Decree on the Apostolate of Lay People,* said simply but emphatically, "The young should become the first apostles of the young." That means that if you are a young man or woman who knows and loves Jesus Christ, then you are called to be a missionary, an apostle, to other people your age.

I don't mean you have to become a great orator, or a preacher, or anything like that. The Lord will use you as you simply live out your Christian life in a dedicated way, and as you share openly and honestly with others what Jesus has done in your life. Don't be afraid to share about him with others. Just be yourself. The Lord will work through your voice, your mind, your heart, as you give yourself to him to be used in evangelism.

I think of this kind of natural, daily-life evangelism in terms of four simple words: prayer, care, dare, share.

First comes *prayer*. Prayer is the indispensable first ingredient in all Christian service, and evangelism is no exception. As someone once said, "It is necessary to talk to God about men before we can talk to men about God."

Many people have told me that there is one prayer God never fails to answer, and that is the request, "Lord, bring me into contact with someone who needs to hear about you." After all, there are millions of people who fit that description! Ask the Lord to bring you into contact with the one person he has especially prepared to respond to your witness and testimony.

But prayer is not important only when *preparing* for evangelism. It's also vital *during* evangelism. Every time you share the gospel with another person, there are really four people involved: you, the other person, the devil (who is trying to undo all your efforts), and the Lord, who works by his Spirit both in you and in the other person. Even as you're speaking, you can ask the Holy Spirit to anoint your words and to open the heart of the person you're with.

Next, it is important that we *care* about the person we're evangelizing. What, after all, is our goal in introducing people to Jesus? To hang more "spiritual scalps" from our belt? To earn a merit badge for chalking up the greatest number of conversions? To impress our friends and youth group leaders with our evangelistic exploits?

Of course not. Our goal is love. Our aim is to *serve* our friends and family, to help them find the answers to the problems that plague them, to help them experience the peace and joy and excitement that we have found in following Christ.

When we care about someone, we naturally want to give them the best of everything, and the very best thing of all is Jesus Christ. He's the greatest gift we can give. A particular greeting card company says its cards are the ones to give "when you care enough to send the very best." May God help us care enough about our friends and acquaintances to want to give *them* the very best: the Lord himself.

The next word is *dare*. All of us experience some amount of timidity or fear when the time comes to talk to another person about Jesus Christ. It's a thoroughly natural, human reaction. We shouldn't be embarrassed by it, and we certainly shouldn't let it stop us from sharing the gospel.

What we need, obviously, is courage. Please note that courage does not mean the absence of fear. Rather, it means the ability to carry on *in spite of* fear. We often think that people are able to be "brave" simply because they never feel afraid. That's not true. Brave people feel just as frightened as you and I do in dangerous or threatening situations. Their courage consists in the ability to press on despite their fear and do what they know needs to be done.

Where does this courage, this ability to press through fear, come from? From the Holy Spirit. "God did not give us a spirit of timidity," Paul reminds his young friend Timothy, "but a spirit of power and love and self-control. Do not be ashamed then of testifying to our Lord" (2 Tm 1:7-8, RSV). Any time timidity makes us hesitant about sharing our faith, we can call on the Holy Spirit within us to give us the boldness we need to press on. We can ask God to make us daring in his service.

Finally, we must *share* our faith with others. You don't need to be a theologian to bring someone to know Jesus. You just need to share with them what you've learned about Jesus and the difference he has made in your life. Very few things are as persuasive as a clear, simple, direct testimony to what God has done for you.

Your primary goal isn't to get someone to agree to a set of theological assertions. Your goal is to get them interested in meeting a *person*. Once someone's interest has been captivated by the person of Jesus and the prospect of getting to know him personally, there'll be plenty of time to explain the key truths and answer whatever questions arise.

Jesus Christ is our hero, our model, our example, our goal. He is the only thing worth living for. And, as someone has said, "If Jesus Christ is worth anything, he's worth everything." Let's decide to give ourselves totally to him and to invite the Holy Spirit to burn within us so that we are always on fire for Jesus.

EIGHT

Voices of Experience

T HIS BOOK HAS COVERED A LOT OF PRINCIPLES. We've talked
about God's love, his forgiveness, his grace. We've talked
about God's wisdom for handling various problem areas.
We've talked about the joy that comes from living for him.

Well, principles are fine, but what most of us want to know
is whether they really work. What do they really look like in
concrete terms? What can they look like in *my* life?

The best way I know to answer those questions is to share
with you how I've seen them work in the lives of two real-life,
flesh-and-blood individuals. We'll see how they struggled with
some tough problems, how God met them in their darkness
and discouragement, and how their lives were changed by his
love and forgiveness and power.

Kevin's Story

"I was in the eighth grade when I discovered the meaning of
life. At least I *thought* I had discovered it. My older brother was
a senior in high school at the time and had been chosen as
'Prom King' at the Senior Prom. Our whole family got to go to
the first part of the prom to see him receive his crown.

"I was awed. He and his date ascended the stage as the band
played and the hundreds of people in the audience applauded.
I thought to myself, 'Someday that's going to be me up there.

75

Someday all these people will be clapping for me. That's what I'm going to live for.'

"I should have known better, of course. Through a rather unusual series of events, I had actually been baptized in the Spirit the year before, and I was trying to follow the Lord. But I didn't stick with it.

"It all went back to my mother. When I was in seventh grade, my mother had gone through a significant conversion experience and had been baptized in the Holy Spirit. At first the whole family was in a mild state of shock over what had happened to her. She instantaneously quit smoking. We thought that was great. She also began saying, 'Praise the Lord,' all the time, putting up religious posters and banners all over the house, and trying to drag all of us to prayer meetings. We thought that was not so great. I remember asking my brother, 'What's the deal with Mom?' He just rolled his eyes and said, 'I don't know, but I don't like it.' That was pretty much the way I felt about it, too.

"But I was still young and impressionable, and eventually Mom's enthusiastic faith rubbed off on me. I went to some prayer meetings, got prayed over to be baptized in the Holy Spirit, and began to pray in tongues. But it didn't last.

"By the time I reached eighth grade, I realized that there was a lot more going on in the world than Mom's prayer meetings. I began to be very aware of what other people thought of me. My experience at my brother's Senior Prom cemented my resolve to pursue popularity at all costs.

"I discovered that one way to become popular in high school was to become known for doing all the things that everyone knew you weren't supposed to do: drinking, smoking dope, having sex. My friends and I found it all too easy to get into those things.

"We started off slowly, but we made rapid progress. I was still in the eighth grade when a group of us went fishing and brought along some beer we swiped from one of our families' refrigerators. We quickly began drinking more and more. At first, we'd go out together and get drunk maybe once a month. Before long we were getting drunk together every weekend.

"But after a while, just getting drunk every week wasn't enough. We started to experiment with marijuana. At first we messed around with some pretty low-grade stuff that someone had grown in their back yard. But by the time I was a junior in high school, we had become fairly sophisticated pot smokers. We had connections with people who could sell us some fairly high-powered and high-priced dope from South America, Hawaii, and so on. I got stoned pretty frequently.

"I felt like my life was coming along nicely. I had a job, so I had plenty of money to spend, and I had a car of my own, so I was able to be independent. Along with all the drinking and the dope-smoking and the carousing came quite a reputation as a hell-raiser, and along with that reputation came a lot of popularity with the kids at school.

"I was only mildly surprised when I was selected to be Senior Prom King, even though I was still only in my junior year. After all, that was what I had been aiming for: popularity, reputation, applause. I had set out to make my dream come true, and now I was seeing it happen.

"But a funny thing happened. On the night of the prom, my date and I ascended the stage just as my brother had done years before. The band played and the people applauded. And I stood there, at what should have been the pinnacle of my life, and found myself feeling utterly dead inside. I thought to myself, 'Is this all there is to it? Is this what I've been looking forward to all these years?' It can be quite a shock to suddenly attain something you've been dreaming of for years, and find out that it isn't all that great, and that you now have nothing left to aim for.

"I was depressed a lot during this time. My dream had been fulfilled, but *I* was still very much unfulfilled. I managed to keep my depression pretty well hidden from the world. On the outside I seemed like my old self. I'd smile and laugh and joke around with my buddies. But inside I was miserable. I had a lot of 'friends,' but I didn't really have a *friend*, someone who really cared about me, someone who liked me not because I had a car and was fun to party with, but just because I was me.

"I was getting high every day. In fact, I was usually getting high four or five times a day. Sometimes I'd smoke dope with my friends, sometimes all by myself. Usually I'd have to go out somewhere to hide what I was doing from my parents, but sometimes when they were gone I'd just get high right there at home. That turned out to be dangerous. It very nearly cost me my life.

"My dad used to own a small handgun, which he kept hidden away in a cupboard above the refrigerator. On several occasions, when I was home alone smoking pot, I'd reach up into that cupboard and take the gun down. I'd empty the bullets from all the chambers but one, spin the drum, cock the hammer, point the gun at my head, and pull the trigger. I can only thank God that I never lost at Russian Roulette.

"At about this time, my parents wanted me to go on a weekend retreat for high school kids called a Search. I wasn't exactly thrilled with the idea. As you can imagine, I had pretty well forgotten about the Lord by this time. My experiences with my mom's prayer group, with praying in tongues and all the rest, were just a distant and slightly embarrassing memory.

"My parents had filled out the application form for the Search—all but the space for my signature. At first they would just leave it lying around my bedroom, hoping that I'd sign it. Then they started 'mentioning' it every so often, 'reminding' me to sign the card so I could go on the retreat. I resisted all their efforts.

"Finally, I got so mad at them for pestering me about the retreat that I ripped up the card and tossed the pieces in the trash. The next day my dad sat me down, set another card in front of me, and told me to sign it. 'Kevin,' he said bluntly, 'whether you like it or not, you are going to go on that retreat.' I'll tell you a secret: that was what I had wanted all along. Though I wouldn't admit it to myself at the time, deep inside I wanted to go on the retreat. I just wanted to be able to tell my friends that my parents had forced me to go.

"As it turned out, a couple of my friends were also going on the Search. I'm afraid that didn't work out very well for the team members. On Friday night we told them we were going out for 'some fresh air.' Actually, we went outside and got high. As often happened, when we got high we got giddy, and we started laughing at everything and everybody. We were sharing a room with a team member, and we drove the poor guy crazy. We found everything he did extraordinarily hilarious. He put his suitcase down on the bed, and we laughed. He hung up his jacket, and we laughed. He combed his hair, and we laughed. We were not very cooperative, to say the least.

"By Saturday morning I had pretty well dug in my heels and decided to be as uncooperative as I could. We'd have small group discussions after the presentations, and I'd do everything I could to wreck them. They'd ask us questions like, 'Who do you wish was here with you, so you could share this weekend with them?' And I'd say, 'Cheryl Tiegs.' I kept up that kind of attitude and behavior through most of the day.

"One of the parts of the retreat was to read some letters that had been sent with us from our parents and other people who knew us. As we were reading them later on Saturday afternoon, I found myself being touched by the ones sent to me, in spite of my efforts to laugh them off. Some of them were from friends of my parents, saying that they thought I was a nice guy and that they loved me. They were very sincere in trying to communicate love to me. I wasn't used to that. There was a similar letter from my father—the first time I could remember getting a letter from him. What touched me most was a note that one of the team members had inserted. He said, 'Kevin, I've noticed you don't like it here. I understand, I really do. I was in the same place last year. If you'd like to talk, I'm here.'

"Those letters were instruments of the Holy Spirit bringing God's love to me. I was suddenly overwhelmed by the realization that God loved me. Not only that, but he forgave me. Of course I'd always known that most of what I was doing with my life was wrong. I had just pushed it out of my mind and refused to think about it. Now it was staring me in the face—the grief I had caused my parents, the damage I had done to myself and others, the sadness I had caused the Lord. But what was also staring me in the face was the fact that God wanted to forgive me, and cleanse me, and help me start fresh.

"It was too much. I hurriedly excused myself, went to the bathroom, sat down, and cried my eyes out. I was in there for hours, bawling like a baby. I was just experiencing the 'hound of heaven,' who had patiently pursued me and had now cornered me and was pouring out his love on me. Finally, in my heart, I cried out, 'Lord, I surrender. I want to live for you. I want to give my life to you and be the person you want me to be and do whatever you want me to do.' And that was that.

"I didn't become perfect overnight. There were still lots of struggles. When I came back from the retreat, all my old friends were still there, expecting me to be the same person I was before. I had a hard time with that. I'd go to parties with them, and on a couple occasions I smoked pot again. But I realized it was wrong and I just didn't want to do it any more. Over a period of a few months I was able to give it up for good.

"Eventually I realized that if I was really going to live for Jesus, I was going to have to break with my former friends. But I was afraid to try to 'go it alone' with the Lord. My whole life had been built around doing things that would make other people like me, and it was hard to think about going ahead with things that I knew others wouldn't understand and probably wouldn't like. In the end, though, God gave me the grace to do it. I just said, 'The heck with it. I'm going to live for Jesus and I don't care what anybody thinks.' I think we have to make that kind of radical break with our past or we'll never get anywhere in the Christian life."

Kevin is right. The Christian life is a radical one, and living it does require a radical break with the sinful life we've left behind. But just as God gave Kevin the grace to make that break, he'll give it to you as well if you turn to him and ask him for it.

Beth's Story

"I don't know how many people realize the enormous need that young people feel for acceptance by their peers. It was a strong driving force in my life when I was in high school. Some aspects of it seem so innocent: being named 'Miss School Spirit,' or being part of the Homecoming Queen's Court. But other parts—the drinking, the drugs, the pressure to get sexually active—are much more dangerous.

"I was in my junior year of high school when I went on what was called an Encounter weekend—short for 'Teens Encounter Christ.' I had a real experience of God on that weekend. For the first time, I felt secure enough in God's love that I was able to resist the pressures to get into drinking or drugs or immoral relationships just in order to be 'cool.'

"But that ability to resist seemed to crumble when I got to college. On campus I encountered an overwhelming drive toward sin and death. Temptations and pressures that had arisen only occasionally in high school seemed to be everywhere in college. If you didn't drink excessively, if you didn't use drugs, if you didn't sleep around, you were considered abnormal.

"I tried to stand on my own, but I didn't succeed very well. I tried to seek fellowship with other Christians, but amid the pressures of studies and social life, I slowly but surely drifted away from the Lord. I reached a point where I just didn't care any more what I did or what happened to me. I can remember looking in a mirror and realizing how hard and corrupt I had become, then just shrugging my shoulders and thinking, 'So what? I'm no different from anyone else. What does it matter?'

"The most devastating thing that happened was when I broke up with a guy whom I thought I was in love with. I couldn't bear the pain, the loneliness, the rejection. I was so far away from the Lord by this time that turning to him in my need didn't even occur to me. Instead, I turned to alcohol. I would go out and get so thoroughly drunk that I couldn't stand up, couldn't think, couldn't feel anything inside. I just wanted to numb myself against the hurt I was feeling.

"That was the condition I was in the night I was raped.

"I knew the guy, though not very well. He just came up to my dorm room, took me to his room, and forced himself on me. I was terrified at what was happening, and I wanted to stop it somehow, but I was too drunk to resist.

"I cannot begin to share with you the depth of pain I felt, the depth of my hatred for him, the depth of my self-hatred. It was as if my entire world—what was left of it by that time—was shattered. Everything I had held as true was no longer the truth. Everyone I had ever trusted, I could no longer trust. It was as if I was surrounded by a thick, black cloud, totally enveloped in darkness.

"I had no desire for anything in life. My girlfriends made me study, but I could never focus my mind on my work. They made me eat, even though I could hardly stand the sight of food. They even had to make me go to sleep, because I was so terrified of the nightmares I kept having.

"I went for counseling. I managed to get over most of my really serious outward problems, and it looked to my counselor as though I were making excellent progress. In one sense, I suppose I was. But I was still empty and hardened inside.

"Eventually I transferred to a Christian school and very, very slowly things began to improve. I turned back to the Lord as best as I could. I had a hard time receiving love from people and a hard time believing God loved me, but gradually, through godly counseling, through meditation on Scripture, through the Sacrament of Reconciliation, and through the Eucharist, God began to break into my life and take away the clouds that surrounded me. It was like someone tearing down an old building that had once housed a dread disease. He threw out the old, contaminated bricks and rebuilt my life from the foundation up.

"The things of this world will pass away, but the love of God will never change. Our plans and dreams will pass away. Our parents and families will pass away. Our friends will pass away. The only stable thing, the only rock-solid, unchanging thing in our lives, is the power of God's love for us. All we need to do is turn to him, and he'll receive us with open arms. And then nothing can ever take his love away from us.

"Today I know that I stand firm in the Lord's love. I had always felt that the worst thing that could ever happen to me would be to be raped, because that so deeply affects the totality of your life. But that, in fact, happened to me, and God brought me through it. Now I know that *nothing* can separate me from the love of God. Nothing that can happen to me can destroy who I am as God's beloved daughter."

I cannot help but be overwhelmed by the goodness and mercy and power of God in rescuing this young man and woman from the terrible darkness in which they were living. Again, that same goodness and mercy and power are available for you.

These stories also illustrate something else: the importance of being supported in our Christian walk by other brothers and sisters who can encourage us in our faith and strengthen us in our continuing obedience to God's word. In the next chapter we'll meet some young people who have experienced the power of that kind of peer support.

We're in It Together

I N CHAPTER SEVEN WE TALKED ABOUT what it means to live our life on fire for Jesus. In it we considered four important elements of such a life: faith, intercession, repentance, and evangelism. But as we saw in the last chapter, there's one more important thing that we should remember, and that's the importance of receiving support and encouragement from others.

Think for a moment about a campfire. It's made up of pieces of wood, and these pieces must be arranged together in the proper way. When the pieces of firewood are placed together, they can all burn brightly. If you pull them apart, though, the individual pieces may keep going for a time, but the flames quickly die down.

The Christian life is the same way. If we're to keep our lives burning brightly for the Lord, we have to stay joined to other brothers and sisters who are also on fire for Jesus. If we try to make it on our own, chances are we'll not last very long. The Christian life is not a do-it-yourself project. We need each other.

Peer support is important if we're to follow through on the four main elements of "fire." We need brothers and sisters to build our faith. We need brothers and sisters to pray with us when we're interceding. We need brothers and sisters to help us see how we may be missing the mark in our walk with the Lord, and to encourage us in our repentance. And we need

85

brothers and sisters to work alongside us in sharing the gospel. Jesus understood this; that's why he always sent the disciples in pairs when they went out to preach.

Earlier in this book we met four young people from Dallas, Texas, who shared with us some of the main problems they see facing young people these days. These four young people are part of a rather highly developed "peer support" situation: a Christian covenant community. It's called the Christian Community of God's Delight, and it's made up of hundreds of people, young and old, married and single, who have decided to live their lives fully for Jesus Christ and to commit themselves to support one another in doing so. Their experience of community life paints a striking picture of the importance of receiving support from our brothers and sisters in Christ.

Fr. John: What does it mean to you to belong to a community, one that involves so many of your parents, relatives, friends?

Mark: It's been a great support group. When you're living out in the world, you see so many different styles of behavior, and sometimes you start to ask yourself, "Why am I so different? Is there something wrong with me?" But then you get back together with brothers and sisters, and you say, "No, what we're doing is right. This is really the best way to live, to live for the Lord."

Sandy: Out in the world the big thing is, "Be yourself. Don't let other people form you." But the fact is, you're being formed by other people all the time. It's not a question of *whether* your values and personality will be influenced by someone else. It's just a question of *which* other people they'll be formed by. Being in community means you're making a choice to be influenced by people who stand for the same things you do. It helps reinforce what you know is right, what you know you want for your life.

Carol: What I have found in community is that I actually *can* "be myself" in that I don't have to worry about what my brothers and sisters think of me. I know they love me—they're committed to love me. I don't have to worry about whether if I do this or that they will stop loving me. If I do well, they love me enough to encourage me. If I mess up, they love me enough to tell me.

That kind of unconditional love is not what most people experience these days.

Carol: I used to worry constantly about whether I was too pushy, or too insensitive, or whatever. I was always looking over my shoulder, wondering whether what I'd just said or done was alright or whether I'd hurt somebody. Well, I'm learning how to handle that better. But the great thing is that in community, there's no fear of losing a friendship over something minor like that, because you know you're bonded together in Christ.

Joe: Another aspect of Christian community is having someone to turn to in difficult times. I experienced this in one of my first classes at college.

College teachers have complete control to teach the principles of whatever the subject is. Their goal is supposed to be to teach things in an objective, unbiased way, but it rarely comes across that way. A lot of the time they are presenting their own beliefs.

In this one particular class we were discussing abortion. The instructor clearly thought abortion is a good thing, and it seemed like everyone in the room agreed with what the instructor was saying.

I had seen other kids who said something that went against what most of the others believed, get ridiculed and torn down. But I got together with a brother from the community, and we talked the whole thing through. Finally I was able to say to myself, this is what God has to say about this issue, and this is what I'm going to stand on. And the next day I got up and said, "I respect your opinion, but I personally see it another way." It was tough but I did it. I never could have done it, though, without that support.

Apart from living with their families in Christian community, these young men and women have experienced Christian peer support in another significant way as well: by attending the special weekend conferences for Christian young people held each summer at The Franciscan University of Steubenville, in Steubenville, Ohio. These conferences bring together thousands of high school and college-age men and women for a weekend of worship, teaching, and fellowship.

What have the summer youth conferences at The University of Steubenville come to mean in your lives?

Sandy: I'll never forget the first one I went to. The second night we were there, I was going downstairs in the dorm to call my parents and tell them what a good time I was having, and I fell down on the stairs and broke my ankle.

I had never experienced so much love from Christian brothers and sisters. Usually I'm the type of person who doesn't want anyone to help me. I'd rather just do it all myself. But for the rest of the weekend, people I'd never even seen before would pick me up and carry me to the sessions and find a chair for me and everything.

After it was all over, and we were all packed up and waiting to get into the vans so we could start for home, we spent some time praying. The whole experience caught up with me and overwhelmed me, and I wept with joy. I didn't want to leave, because I had experienced so much of God's love through the people there. I'll never forget that, the love they all showed me. It was so real and so strong.

Isn't it true that when we meet brothers and sisters in the Lord the Holy Spirit seems to create instant friendships? We don't have to struggle to give or receive love, because the love of God is with us. How about some of the rest of you? What has been your experience at the conferences?

Mark: Something that the Steubenville conference has always done for me is to confirm the unity that we have in Jesus. I knew some Christian friends in the community, and I knew a few kids at school who were good Christians, but my viewpoint ended there. Going to Steubenville and meeting so many people from all over the country, and all of them wonderful Christians, made me feel confident that we're not alone back home, that there are lots of other Christians out there that we can be united with.

Carol: When we were all gathered under that big tent, you couldn't help but feel the presence of the Lord. Even those who came with a negative attitude couldn't help but sense it.

One of the men who was speaking had us all say out loud that we loved the Lord and wanted to dedicate our lives to him. That really made you think. You often say to yourself, "Sure, I love the Lord." But to say it out loud and have everyone else hear you say it—it really hits you. It drives home to you that you really *do* love the Lord and you really *do* want to live for him.

Joe: I went to my first Steubenville conference as a team member for our youth ministry. God really used the young people I went with to touch my life and to reveal his love to me more fully. The change I saw in them between the ride up there and through the conference to the ride home was just incredible.

I especially remember one night, after everything was over, two or three members of our youth group began praying with one another. Nothing real dramatic, just holding hands and praying. Slowly but surely, more kids showed up, until everyone from our group was there, and they were just praying over everybody. Tears were flowing like Niagara Falls. I could stand back and look over the whole situation and just feel the love radiating from the group. I think the Lord really worked in me through the whole experience, and his love is stronger in me now as a result.

What's the main lesson you've learned at the conference, the main point that has stayed with you?

Mark: I've never forgotten a talk that someone gave about the gospel story of the treasure hidden in the field. I'd always thought of it as a nice story but had never seen any personal application in it for me. But the way it was presented emphasized that the man who found the treasure sold *everything* he had, and that he bought *the whole field*. He didn't just buy the treasure and carry it off. He bought the whole field, the treasure and everything that comes with it.

What that said to me was that when I give my life to Jesus I have to accept it all, the whole package, not just the parts that look appealing to me. I have to accept the things that take some effort. Like really getting down to brass tacks and taking my prayer time and doing my Scripture reading because I need that to grow, and sometimes it doesn't just come naturally to want to do it.

But I also find that all my brothers and sisters are also "in the field." They come with the treasure, too, and they help me to keep my focus on it and to do the things I know I need to do, even when it's not easy.

The main thing that strikes me from this conversation is the constant reference to how these young people experience love and acceptance from one another. When they are together as followers of the Lord Jesus Christ, they are sons and daughters of the king. They are royalty! And they treat each other like royalty.

That's important because you and I both know how many young people don't experience being treated that way by their friends, and who don't experience that kind of love and acceptance. Maybe they're not star athletes. Maybe they're not on the cheerleading team. Maybe they're not at the head of the class academically. Maybe they're not physically attractive, or don't own a car, or don't wear fancy clothes to school. There are so many ways we have of excluding those who don't "measure up" on some scale that the world says is important.

But we don't need any more young people trapped on the outside. We don't need any more young people crying themselves to sleep at night because of the loneliness and rejection they experience all day. We don't need any more young people copping out with booze and drugs, or trying to become popular by becoming sexually promiscuous, or just tuning out the world around them and retreating into a shell of isolation and alienation.

We need young men and women who remember that we're in it together—who watch out for one another, who care for one another, who pray with one another, who call one another on to holiness, who encourage and support and accept one another. And we need young people who reach out to those around them, who by their example and by their spoken testimony witness to the life-changing power of Jesus Christ.

It's also important that we not see evangelism as simply an individual project. Evangelism works best when young people can come together with other young people in a positive, God-centered environment where they can study Scripture together, pray together, and even just talk together about the things that are really important in their lives.

Many times adults can be instrumental in helping to form this kind of environment; parents, teachers, and youth ministers can all play key roles in the process. If you know people who are already working to bring about this kind of peer support group, pitch in and help them.

But what if you're not in a situation like that? What if there is no youth group in your church or prayer group, and no organized circle of Christians where you go to school?

In that case, I think it's a safe bet that the Lord may want to start with *you*. If you are a young man or young woman who loves Jesus Christ, and if you know of even one other young man or woman who loves Jesus Christ, then I believe the Lord wants you to take the initiative to join together with that brother or sister and begin to create a peer support system that encourages faith and holiness.

God can do great things even through such humble beginnings. There's tremendous power available when young people join together to love and serve Jesus Christ. I've seen it happen at The University of Steubenville, where I teach. By regularly focusing on preaching the gospel and helping students come together in peer support groups that help them sustain and deepen their Christian commitment, we've seen those students have an increasingly significant impact on the life of the entire university.

In fact, after several years of this, we've actually come to a point where the majority of students on campus are on fire for Jesus. As a result, a funny thing has happened. In most places in the world, it's the dedicated Christians who feel different from the crowd, who feel awkward or embarrassed. But at Steubenville, it's just the other way around. There it's the other students, the ones who haven't yet fully committed their lives to the Lord, who sometimes feel a bit awkward. It's peer pressure in reverse, working for the Lord's purposes instead of against them.

The same thing can happen in your situation. It makes a difference when young people come together as a group and say, "We believe the gospel, and we want to live according to the way of faith, love, and purity." You can make a difference in your high school, in your church, in whatever youth sub-culture you happen to be part of. It starts when you make the decision to be an all-out disciple of the Lord Jesus Christ. It grows when you join with others who've made the same decision, or invite them to join with you. It's like a campfire: the more logs you throw on it, the higher and hotter the flames will burn!

TEN

An Open Letter

R ADIO ANNOUNCER PAUL HARVEY HAS A DAILY FEATURE THAT I enjoy a lot. It's called "The Rest of the Story." In it, he relates an anecdote involving some famous person or incident from the past. But he purposely keeps some of the details vague, so that you're not sure who or what he's talking about. Finally he drops the pretense and reveals the identity of his subject. "And now," he concludes, "you know *the rest of the story.*"

I have just that kind of story to tell about a man who felt called by the Lord to work with young people. Because I've put so much of my own time and energy into working with young people over the years, I have a special place in my heart for youth ministers. The story of this particular youth minister has always inspired me, because his experience shows the tremendous rewards that this kind of work can bring.

This youth minister—his name was John, though that's not really important—lived in a part of the world and during a time in history when there was nothing around him but war, poverty, and oppression. He was a Christian living under a godless military regime that had occupied his country and all but outlawed the practice of religion.

John was still a rather young man, but he had already witnessed the cruel dismantling of his native culture. He had watched as one freedom after another was stripped away by the

government. All around him was discouragement and disillu-
sionment and despair, especially among the young, who had
simply lost hope in everything.

He himself was a simple man. He was not well-educated, not
widely traveled, not what we would call worldly-wise. Because
of the pressing situation of his family, he had dropped out of
school to work in his father's tailor shop.

But John loved Jesus Christ, and he loved young people. He
loved them with a depth of compassion that could only come
from a life lived deeply in the Spirit of God. He longed to see
them set free from their despair. Even more than their
economic poverty, he longed to see them freed from their
spiritual poverty.

The regime had taken away his external freedoms, but it
could not stifle his inner freedom. Even though it was against
the law, John would hold secret meetings in his apartment and
share his faith with a group of young men who took the risk of
attending. For many months the meetings continued. Some
weeks his apartment was crowded, and other weeks it was
nearly empty as young people came and went. Occasionally he
saw signs of progress. More often he found himself colliding
head-on with the emptiness and despair that characterized so
many young people. But he pressed on.

Before long his attention was drawn to one young man who
had only recently started to attend the secret meetings. He
knew the young man had suffered much. He was only twenty
years old and already he was alone in the world: his mother, his
father, his sister, and his brother had all died. He had dropped
out of school himself when the government forbade him to
pursue his chosen line of study. His entire world seemed to
have collapsed.

But John could detect in him signs of strong character and
leadership ability. He sensed that here, beneath the layers of
misery and loneliness, lay one of God's jewels. If only he could
get through to this young man! If only he could help him see

the light of the gospel!

John began to take the lonely young man under his wing. He spent time with him. He taught him what little he knew about theology. Mostly, he simply shared with this young man his own spiritual life.

The effect was gradual, but unmistakable. The young man responded to the light of faith he could see glowing deep within John's heart. As a result of John's caring, his witness, his imparting of faith and hope and vision, a whole new world opened up before this young man.

A short time later their paths parted, never to cross again. But the young man never forgot the simple, faith-filled "older brother" who had done so much to help him. He spoke of him often as the years went by.

As I mentioned before, the youth minister's name was John. He's not very well known. But the young man he took under his wing? You've almost certainly heard of *him*. His name is Karol Wojtila, better known these days as Pope John Paul II.

And now you know the rest of the story!

I suppose it was that life-changing experience during his own youth that has given John Paul II such a strong interest in young people. Wherever he goes on his many travels around the world, however large the throngs that press in around him, he somehow always seems drawn, like a magnet, to the young. He likes to talk with them, to laugh with them, just be with them.

He also likes to share with them the same light of faith that his friend John shared with him so many years ago. One of his favorite themes is the gospel story of Jesus' encounter with the rich young ruler. In fact, he has written his reflections on this story into an open letter, "To the Youth of the World." In it, he calls young men and women to make a radical commitment of their lives to the cause of Christ and the service of the gospel. I'd like to share that letter with you:

To the Youth of the World:

A letter from Pope John Paul II in shortened format

" 'Always be prepared to make a defense to anyone who calls you to account for the hope that is in you' (1 Pt 3:15). This is the exhortation that I address to you young people in this United Nations International Youth Year.

"We are looking to you, for all of us, thanks to you, in a certain sense continually become young again. So your youth is not just your personal property or the property of a generation. It is a special possession belonging to everyone.

"This message of the Apostle Peter, to 'be prepared,' was given to the very first generation of Christians. It has a relationship to the whole of the Gospel of Jesus Christ. Perhaps we shall see this relationship more clearly when we meditate upon Christ's conversation with the young man, as recorded by the evangelists (Mt 19:16-22; Mk 10:17-22; Lk 18:18-23).

"To the question: 'Good teacher, what must I do to inherit eternal life?' Jesus replies first with the question: 'Why do you call me good? No one is good but God alone.' Then he goes on: 'You know the Commandments: "Do not kill, Do not commit adultery, Do not steal, Do not bear false witness, Do not defraud, Honor your father and mother." ' Jesus thus reminds his questioner of some of the Commandments.

" 'Teacher, all these things I have observed from my youth.' Then, writes the evangelist, 'Jesus looking upon him loved him, and said to him. "You lack one thing; go, sell what you have, and give to the poor, and you will have treasure in heaven; and come, follow me." '

"At this point the atmosphere of the meeting changes. The evangelist writes that 'at that saying his face fell, and he went away sorrowful; for he had great possessions.'

"One can say that these words contain a particularly

profound truth about youth. Permit me therefore to link my reflections mainly to this meeting and this Gospel text. Perhaps in this way it will be easier for you to develop your own conversation with Christ—a conversation which is of fundamental importance.

Youth Is a Special Treasure

"We shall begin with the end. The young man goes away sorrowful, 'for he had great possessions.' Perhaps this is the situation of some, but it is not typical. Another way to put the matter is that youth is *in itself* (independently of any material good) *a special treasure* of a young man or woman.

"For the period of youth is the time of a particularly intense discovery of the human 'I' and of the properties and capacities connected with it. Gradually a unique potentiality is revealed, in which there is inscribed a plan of a future life. Life presents itself as the carrying-out of that plan: as 'self-fulfillment.'

"The treasure which is youth reveals itself as the treasure of discovering and at the same time of organizing, choosing, foreseeing and making the first personal decisions, decisions that will be important for the future in the strictly personal dimension of human existence. At the same time, these decisions are of considerable social importance. The young man in the Gospel was precisely in this phase, as we can deduce from his questions.

"Does the treasure of youth necessarily turn a person *from* Christ? The evangelist does not say this. Rather, the text leads us to a different conclusion. The decision to go away from Christ was influenced by the young man's possessions, *not by what he was!* What he *was,* a young man, had *led* him to Jesus. And it had also impelled him to ask those questions which in the clearest way concern the plan for the whole of life. What must I do? What must I do so that my life may have full value and full meaning?

"The youth of each one of you is a treasure that is manifested precisely in these questions. People ask such questions throughout life. But in the time of youth they are particularly urgent. You ask yourselves these questions sometimes with impatience, and at the same time you yourselves understand that the reply cannot be hurried or superficial. They are questions that embrace the whole of human existence.

God Is Love

"Christ's reply to the young man is 'No one is good but God alone.' The young man's question had been: How must I act so that my life will have meaning and value? Christ's answer means this: Only God is the ultimate basis of all values; only he gives the definitive meaning to our human existence. In him and him alone do values find their authenticity.

"Why is God alone good? Because he is love. Christ gives this answer in the words of the Gospel, and above all by the witness of his own life and death: 'For God so loved the world that he gave his only Son' (Jn 3:16). God is good precisely because he 'is love' (1 Jn 4:8, 16).

"When you are tested by personal suffering, or become profoundly aware of the suffering of others; when you experience shock at the sight of the many kinds of evil that exist in the world; finally, when you come face to face with the mystery of sin, Christ's reply is this: 'Only God is good.' This reply may seem difficult, but at the same time it is firm and it is true. How I pray that you, my young friends, will hear Christ's reply in the most personal way possible; that you will find the interior path which enables you to grasp it, accept it and undertake its accomplishment.

"Your youth opens different prospects before you; it offers you as a task the plan for the whole of your lives. Hence the question about values; hence the question about the meaning of life, about truth, about good and evil. When Christ in his reply to you tells you to refer all this to God, at the same time he shows you that the source and foundation of this is in yourselves. For each one of you is the image and likeness of God through the very act of creation (Gn 1:26). This image and likeness makes you put the questions that you must ask yourselves.

The Question about Eternal Life

"How will my life have value and meaning? Is this earnest question intelligible to the people of today? Are we not the generation whose horizon of existence is completely filled by earthly progress? If we go beyond the limits of our planet, we do so in order to launch interplanetary flights, transmit signals to the other planets and send cosmic probes in their direction.

"All this has become the content of our modern civilization. Science together with technology has discovered humanity's possibilities with regard to matter, and has also succeeded in dominating the interior world of thoughts, capacities, tendencies and passions.

"But at the same time it is clear that, when we place ourselves in the presence of Christ, we cannot put the question differently from how that young man put it: 'What must I do to inherit eternal life?' Any other question about the meaning and value of our life would be, in the presence of Christ, insufficient and inessential.

"If you wish to talk to Christ, you must on the one hand 'love the world'—for God 'So loved the world that he gave his only Son' (Jn 3:16)—and at the same time you must acquire interior detachment with regard to all this rich and fascinating reality that makes up 'the world.' Christianity teaches us to understand temporal existence from the perspective of eternal life. Without eternal life, temporal existence, however rich, however developed in all aspects, in the end brings us nothing other than the necessity of death.

"Now death seems far distant from youth. And it is. But since youth means the plan for the whole of life—the plan drawn up in accordance with the yardstick of meaning and value—during youth too it is essential to ask the question about the end. So ask Christ, like the young man in the Gospel: 'What must *I* do to inherit eternal life?'

On Morality and Conscience

"Jesus replies to this question: 'You know the Command-ments,' and he lists some of them. The young man who speaks to Christ naturally knows by heart the Commandments; indeed, he can declare with joy: 'All these things I have observed from my youth.' We presume that in the dialogue which Christ is having with each of you, the question is repeated: 'Do you know the Commandments?' It *will* be repeated without fail because the Commandments form part of the Covenant between God and humanity.

"The Commandments determine the essential bases of behavior and decide the moral value of human acts. The culmination of our code of morality is found in the Gospel: in the Sermon on the Mount and in the Commandment of Love.

"At the same time this code of morality is written in yet another form. It is inscribed in the moral conscience of humanity, in such a way that those who do not know the Commandments still find them written on their hearts (Rom 2:15).

"Dear young friends, Christ asks *you* about the state of your moral awareness, and at the same time he questions you about the state of your conscience. This is the fundamental question of your youth, one that concerns your whole plan of life.

Jesus, Looking Upon Him, Loved Him'

"Examining Christ's conversation with the young man, we now enter a new and decisive phase. The young man has heard what he must do and he knows that his life journey to this point coincides with Christ's response. How I hope that the life of each one of you up to this point has similarly coincided with Christ's response! Indeed, it is my hope that your youth will provide you with a sturdy basis of sound principles, that your conscience will attain a mature clear-sightedness that will enable each one of you to remain always a person of conscience, a person of principles, a person who inspires trust; in other words, a person who is credible.

"The moral personality formed in this way is the most important contribution that you can make to life in the community, to the family, to society, to professional activity and also to cultural and political activity, and finally to the community of the Church—to all those spheres with which you are already or will one day be connected.

"Here the Commandments of the Decalogue and of the Gospel take on a decisive meaning, especially the Commandment of Love which opens the human person to God and neighbor. For charity is the 'bond of perfection' (Col 3:14). This evangelical moral code is confirmed by the whole history of humanity, even in ancient times. Confucius, the Japanese master Dengyo Daishi, Mahatma Gandhi—all these moved their followers toward respect for the other person and expressed the principle of not doing to that person what one would not wish done to oneself.

"I hope that, after you have discerned the essential questions for your youth, you will experience what the Gospel means when it says: 'Jesus, looking upon him, loved him.' May you experience a look like that! May you experience the truth that he, Christ, looks upon you with love! At the beginning of Creation, God saw that 'it was very good' (Gn 1:31). That first look of the Creator is reflected in the look of Christ which accompanies his conversation with the young man in the Gospel.

"I think that you will experience this look of Christ in all its depth when you need it most: perhaps in suffering, perhaps with the witness of a pure conscience, as with the young man, or perhaps precisely in an opposite situation: together with the sense of guilt, such as Peter knew when he had three times denied his master. We need such a loving look.

'Follow Me'

"Christ's look of love was a turning point in the conversation. In Matthew's account, the young man asked a new question: 'What do I still lack?' This is a very important question. It shows that in the moral conscience of a young person who is forming the plan for his or her whole life, there is hidden an aspiration to 'something more.'

"When the young man asks about the more: 'What do I still lack?' Jesus looks upon him with love, and this love finds here a new meaning. Humanity is carried interiorly, by the hand of the Holy Spirit, from a life according to the Commandments to a life in the awareness of the gift of love. And Jesus says: 'If you would be perfect, go, sell what you possess and give to the poor, and you will have treasure in heaven; and come, follow me.'

"These words in the Gospel certainly concern the priestly or religious vocation; but at the same time they help us to understand more deeply the question of vocation in a still wider and more fundamental sense.

"One could speak here of the 'life' vocation, which in a way is identical with that plan of life which each of you draws up in the period of your youth. But 'vocation' means something more than 'plan.' During youth, a person puts the question 'What must I do?' not only to himself or herself and to other people from whom an answer can be expected, especially parents and teachers, but to God as Creator and Parent. What must I do? What is your creative plan? What is your will? I wish to do it.

"Little by little, each of you will recognize the talents which you have. When you begin to use them in a creative way you increase them. We can say that youth is the time for discerning talents. I hope that all of you will discover yourselves along the paths of human activity, work and creativity. I hope that you will set out with interest, diligence and enthusiasm.

The Great Challenge of the Future

"This world you are living in will be yours tomorrow. So you rightly ask: Why does humanity's great progress in mastering the material world turn against humanity itself in so many ways? Is this state of affairs irreversible? Can it be changed? Shall we succeed in changing it?

"This is how your conversation with Christ goes on, the conversation begun one day in the Gospel. That young man asked: 'What must I do to have eternal life?' And you put the same question in the style of the times in which it is your turn to be young. 'What must we do to ensure that life—the flourishing life of the human family—will not be turned into the graveyard of nuclear death? What must we do to avoid being dominated by the sin of universal injustice? Will we be able to do it?'

"Christ answers you as he answered the young people of the first generation of the Church through the words of John: 'You are *strong*, and the word of God abides in you' (1 Jn 2:13-14). These words have the strength of the experience of the Cross and Resurrection of Christ, the experience of the apostles, and of the generations of Christians that followed them.

"You *are* strong! You will succeed in getting at the hidden workings of evil, its sources, and thus you will gradually succeed in changing the world, making it more human, more fraternal—and at the same time more of God.

"So, my young friends, I hand you this letter which continues the Gospel conversation of Christ with the young man. We are praying that—against the background of the difficult times in which we live—you 'may always be prepared to make a defense to anyone who calls you to account for the hope that is in you.' Yes, on you depends the future, on you depends also the end of this millennium and the beginning of the next. So do not be passive; take up your responsibilities— in all the fields open to you in our world!"

ELEVEN

Do Not Say,
"I Am Only a Youth"

P OPE JOHN PAUL ENDS HIS LETTER to young people with a
rather bold statement: "On you depends the future, on
you depends also the end of this millennium and the beginning
of the next." That's a heavy burden of responsibility and a stiff
challenge.

I know people are always telling you that you are "the hope
of the future." But that's not just a cliche. It's the truth. You are
indeed the hope of the future—for the Lord, for the church,
for the world. You're the only future we have!

This book has discussed the many problems and difficulties
that face young people today, and I've said that in the power of
the Holy Spirit you can meet all the challenges involved in
serving Jesus Christ and helping establish his kingdom.

But some of you aren't convinced. Some of you are saying in
your hearts, "Come on. I'm just a kid. What can I do?"

That's a very common reaction. In fact, it's one that God has
had to deal with on more than a few occasions.

For example, take the prophet Jeremiah. Jeremiah was one
of the most important prophets in the history of the Jewish
nation. Over the course of several decades, and through the
reigns of many kings, he fearlessly spoke the word the Lord

gave him, calling Israel to repent and warning of judgment if they did not.

He paid the price for speaking this often unpopular message, too: at one point in his life he was abandoned in a cistern and left for dead, and the official records of his messages were destroyed. But God delivered him from death, and the quick thinking of his servant Baruch preserved his prophetic messages for later generations.

Jeremiah was only a young man—perhaps no older than you—when the Lord called him to his life of prophetic service. We know this because Jeremiah himself describes how intimidated he felt when God summoned him. Read carefully this account of God's call and Jeremiah's hesitant response:

Now the word of the Lord came to me saying, "Before I formed you in the womb I knew you, and before you were born I consecrated you; I appointed you a prophet to the nations." Then I said, "Ah, Lord God! Behold, I do not know how to speak, for I am only a youth." But the Lord said to me, "Do not say, 'I am only a youth'; for to all to whom I send you you shall go, and whatever I command you you shall speak. Be not afraid of them, for I am with you to deliver you, says the Lord." Then the Lord put forth his hand and touched my mouth; and the Lord said to me, "Behold, I have put my words in your mouth. See, I have set you this day over nations and over kingdoms, to pluck up and to break down, to destroy and to overthrow, to build and to plant." (Jer 1:4-10, RSV)

When God first calls him and sets before him the task he is to undertake, Jeremiah responds just the way many of us do: "Who, *me*? Are you kidding? They'll never listen to me. I'm too young. I'm just a kid. You'd better find somebody else."

And God's response to Jeremiah is also his response to us: "Yes, *you*. Don't give me any of this 'I'm just a kid' business. I know what I'm doing. I'll stand behind you. You just go out there and do what I tell you to do. Leave the rest to me, and everything will be fine."

In other words, being young is no excuse, in God's eyes, for not growing in holiness. It's no excuse for meekly following the crowd. It's no excuse for not helping turn your home, your school, your neighborhood, upside down for Jesus.

That's what he's called you to. As I understand the message of Scripture, it's those of us who are followers of Jesus Christ who are supposed to be the leaders in the world. It says we are to shine like lights in the darkness of the world. It says we are to be the salt of the earth. It doesn't say we're supposed to be namby-pamby, wishy-washy, Caspar Milquetoast types, always stepping aside and letting others walk off with everything. It says we're supposed to work ourselves into positions where we can cooperate with God in establishing his reign.

If that's what he's called you to do, then you can be sure he'll stand behind you as you do it. You just get out there and do what you know he wants you to do, and watch his Holy Spirit go to work!

For another example, take Timothy, the young man Paul had raised up to care for the fledgling church in Ephesus. Again, we do not know his precise age, but it seems clear he was also rather young. At least, he was young enough that he frequently felt inadequate because of his lack of age and experience. Paul had to encourage him on this point several times. On one such occasion, Paul spelled out just how a young person can have a major impact on the whole church:

Let no one look down on you because of your youth, but be a continuing example of love, faith, and purity to believers. Until I arrive, devote yourself to the reading of Scripture, to preaching and teaching. Do not neglect the gift you received when, as a result of prophecy, the presbyters laid their hands on you. Attend to your duties; let them absorb you, so that everyone may see your progress. (1 Tm 4:12-15)

Consider the wide range of opportunities that Paul indicates are open to young men and women in the body of Christ.
They can proclaim God's word. They can preach the gospel
and call others on to greater holiness. They can be called upon
for special roles of service for which the Holy Spirit has
anointed and appointed them. And, most of all, they can serve
as an example to all—young and old alike—of such crucial
qualities as love, faith, and purity (and, I might add, of all the
other qualities that Paul elsewhere calls "the fruit of the
Spirit"—see, for example, Gal 5:22-23).

The history of the church is filled with the stories of young
people like Jeremiah and Timothy—young men and women
no older, no more experienced, no better educated than you,
who nevertheless accomplished great things for God by simply
trusting and obeying Jesus Christ in the circumstances in
which they found themselves.

—Joseph was only seventeen when God revealed to him that
he was to become the leader of his people (see Gn 37:1-11).

—Samuel was just a baby when his mother Hannah
dedicated him to the Lord, and was only a boy when the Lord
spoke to him in the night and called him to be a prophet (see 1
Sm 1-3).

—David was a young shepherd boy when God singled him
out to become king of Israel and sent him into battle against
Goliath (see 1 Sm 16:1-13; 17:12-58).

—Mary was but a young girl when God called her to become
the mother of our Lord Jesus Christ (see Lk 1:26-38).

In addition, many of the great saints accomplished great
things for God while still in their youth: Francis of Assisi,
Clare of Assisi, Therese of Liseuix, Aloysius Gonzaza, Maria
Govette and Dominic Savio; to name just a few.

I'd like to conclude this book by telling you the story of
some other young people. Their names are not as familiar to us
as the names of the young people in the Bible and among the
saints. But their stories represent the most heroic examples I

know of all-out faithfulness to the Lord. I learned about them when I was researching a television series about the spread of Christianity in Japan.

Christianity came to the shores of Japan through the courageous missionary work of St. Francis Xavier, in the 1500's. From very meager beginnings, his work grew until there was a thriving Christian element among the Japanese people. Before long, this new development came to the attention of the Japanese rulers. They recognized in the Christian faith, with its insistence on the worship of God alone and on loyalty to him alone, a powerful threat to their own authority. They decided to stamp out this new religious phenomenon.

What better way to do it, they thought, than to make an example of some of the more zealous adherents of the new faith? When people saw that becoming a follower of Jesus Christ could lead to suffering, humiliation, even death, maybe then they'd think twice before running after this strange new God.

They selected twenty-six men from the Catholic churches that had been established in several villages on the southern island of Kyoto. For days they forced them to march through the rugged countryside, giving them just enough food and water to keep them alive. Constantly they taunted them and tried to get them to renounce Christ: "Why put yourself through all this? You can still save your life. Deny Jesus Christ and live!" But the twenty-six held firm in their faith.

The end of the forced march came at a small village by the sea. There, on a hill overlooking the ocean, they saw them: twenty-six crosses silhouetted against the sky. "This was how your Master died, was it not?" taunted the guards. "It is how you, too, will die unless you renounce him." But the twenty-six stood firm, and they were led away to be crucified.

I described these brave martyrs as "twenty-six men." But that is not strictly accurate. Five of them were actually boys.

John (they had all taken biblical names when they were

converted) was one of these. Like the others, he could have saved himself from execution by denying his faith. But his heart had been set on fire by stories he had been told of the martyrs who were members of the Society of Jesus. Now God was giving him the opportunity to join his Jesuit heroes in making the ultimate witness to his faith.

John had, in fact, been preparing to seek admission to the order. A few hours before his martyrdom, the Jesuit superior—who was also among the twenty-six, received his vows and accepted him into the Society.

As John went to the cross, a priest next to him encouraged him not to weaken in faith, or to lose heart. He needn't have worried. John turned to him and said, "Father, do not be concerned for me. With God's help, I shall persevere."

And persevere he did. John died, a Jesuit martyr, at the age of nineteen.

Gabriel was a page in the household of one of the local civil officials. All the other young people who served in the household ridiculed him because of his faith and tried to persuade him to abandon it. He, in turn, would invite them to the monastery where he prayed regularly, and urge them to give their lives to Christ.

Gabriel's parents were not Christians. As the persecution of Christians grew more intense, they increasingly feared for their son's life. They brought him back into their home, pleading with him to renounce Christ and save his life. In the end, Gabriel converted his father to Christianity. They were crucified side by side among the twenty-six.

Gabriel, like John, was nineteen when he gave his life for Christ.

Thomas was another who hung on a cross next to his father. They had both been dragged out of their homes, with their distraught mother pleading for mercy. When his body was taken down from the cross, they found tucked in his sleeve a letter Thomas had written to his mother.

In the letter Thomas tells his mother not to worry about him and his father because they are going to heaven, and will wait there for her to join them. He hopes she will come to join them soon. He tells her she must fear sin very much, since sin caused the Lord much suffering; if she does sin, she must confess it and ask the Lord's forgiveness. She must remember that the pleasures of this world appear like a dream and fade away to nothing as a dream does. If anyone persecutes her, she must love them as Jesus did on Calvary. He asks her to take care of his little brother and tells her he will pray for her.

Thomas was fifteen years old.

Anthony's parents, unlike Thomas's, were not Christians. They could not understand, let alone rejoice in, his sufferings for the sake of Christ. They stood at the foot of Anthony's cross and wept bitterly as he died. Pitying them in their sorrow and confusion, Anthony called out to them, "Do not weep because I am hanging from a cross. Soon I shall see God in heaven, where I will remember you. Do not weep! Let the others see that you rejoice because your child is suffering for Jesus Christ, whom he loves more than life."

Anthony was martyred at the age of thirteen.

At the very end of the row stood the smallest of the twenty-six crosses. It belonged to the smallest of the twenty-six martyrs, whose name was Louis.

A nobleman on the island of Kyoto was moved with pity at the sight of little Louis being led to the cross. He pleaded with the boy to change his mind and renounce Christ. "Please listen to me. This is so foolish. You are so young. Come with me. I will take care of you. I will employ you in my house. Please, I beg you, come and join me."

Louis turned to him and said, "It would be better for you to join me in the paradise to which I am going."

The twenty-six were lashed to their crosses. Before each one stood two imperial guards with javelins. At the signal, the two guards were to charge forward and plunge their lances into the heart of the man in front of them. The signal was given. As the javelins pierced his body, Louis was heard to cry out, "Heaven! Jesus! Mary!"

He was twelve years old.

As the writer of the letter to the Hebrews says, "Since we for our part are surrounded by this cloud of witnesses, let us lay aside every encumbrance of sin which clings to us and persevere in running the race which lies ahead." And how do we run that race? "Let us keep our eyes fixed on Jesus, who inspires and perfects our faith. For the sake of the joy which lay before him he endured the cross, heedless of its shame. He has taken his seat at the right hand of the throne of God. Remember how he endured the opposition of sinners; hence do not grow despondent or abandon the struggle" (Heb 12: 1-3).

The age of the saints, and the age of the martyrs, is not ended. There are among us, even today, living saints, heroes of the faith, who will endure the opposition of sinners and run the race with their eyes fixed on Jesus. There are among us, even today, men and women who will be called to make the ultimate witness to faith in Christ by dying a martyr's death. Like their Lord, for the sake of the joy that lies before them they will endure suffering and death, thinking nothing of the shame.

And I believe that there are among us, even today, *young* men and women who are prepared to live lives of radical commitment to our Lord Jesus Christ, who are prepared to say, as did Isaiah, the prophet, "Here I am, send me!" (Is 6:8).

Will you be one of them?

Prayer of Commitment

Lord Jesus Christ, Risen Savior, King of Kings, Son of God, Son of man, I come before you just as I am, acknowledging my sinfulness and my personal weaknesses.

Without you I am nothing, with you, I have everything.

Oh Master, I ask for an increase in faith, hope and love. With praise and thanksgiving I place before you the following needs. (*Here ask for whatever you need, little or big, spiritual or material. Don't hesitate to ask Jesus for anything... He loves you.*)

O Risen Lord, I offer you my life and I truly accept you as my Lord and my God. I surrender to you as my personal Savior and I repent of my sins. I am sorry for having offended you. I unite my sufferings with yours on the cross and I ask to be more deeply unified with you in your Resurrection.

Give me good health in body, soul and spirit. Let your Holy Spirit dwell within my heart. Allow me to experience your Father's love. As you lived with Mary and Joseph, so live within my home and bless every member of my family. I declare you the Lord of my house and ask for the protection of your Precious Blood over my loved ones.

I love you, Jesus Christ; I praise you, Lord. I shall follow you as your disciple every day of my life. Through your Spirit, your Bible, and your Church, teach me your ways. I desire to live in you, with you, for you and through you, my Risen Lord, now and forever. Amen.

FR. JOHN BERTOLUCCI, internationally know Catholic evangelist, joins his efforts with those of The Franciscan University of Steubenville and its affiliated outreach ministries. Under the direction of the university's president, Fr. Michael Scanlan, T.O.R., the university stands committed to providing the resources for young people to pursue their college education in a vibrant, Catholic Christian environment where academic, spiritual, social, and athletic opportunities are available to all students desiring an integrated life on campus.

For his part, Fr. John serves as Associate Professor of Theology, complementing a faculty dedicated to preparing young men and women to enter professional careers with the academic background and Christian character necessary to make an impact on society for Jesus Christ. The 1200-member student body, representing every state and more than twelve foreign countries, work toward graduate and undergraduate degrees in twenty-eight fields of study. Majors range from traditional programs like mathematics and biology to professional programs such as nursing and computer science.

A genuine concern for students beyond the classroom has led to the formation of Christian "households" within the resident halls, providing a dynamic way of living through positive peer support among students. Highly participative student-led organizations have been instrumental in the spiritual growth and formation of hundreds of young people.

Every summer the University's Christian Outreach Center hosts a series of programs to provide leadership, training, and teaching to Catholics seeking a deeper personal relationship with Jesus Christ. Among the specific conferences held are those directed to high school age youth, young adults, and youth ministers.

In addition to its academic and formational dimensions on

campus, the university responds to the challenge of church renewal by serving as home base for a number of Catholic outreaches, including the St. Francis Association for Catholic Evangelism (F.A.C.E.); F.I.R.E., a Catholic alliance of Faith, Intercession, Repentance, and Evangelism; and *New Covenant* magazine.

If you would like more information on the university's academic programs, Christian conferences, or other affiliated outreach ministries, please write to:

Fr. John Bertolucci
P.O. Box 8000
Steubenville, OH 43952
or call: (614) 283-3771